Momma
CUSSES

Momma
CUSSES

A FIELD GUIDE TO

RESPONSIVE PARENTING & TRYING NOT TO BE THE REASON YOUR KID NEEDS THERAPY

GWENNA LAITHLAND

ST. MARTIN'S
ESSENTIALS
NEW YORK

First published in the United States by St. Martin's Essentials, an imprint of St. Martin's Publishing Group

MOMMA CUSSES. Copyright © 2024 by Gwenna Laithland. All rights reserved. Printed in the United States of America. For information, address St. Martin's Publishing Group, 120 Broadway, New York, NY 10271.

www.stmartins.com

The Library of Congress Cataloging-in-Publication Data is available upon request.

ISBN 978-1-250-88266-0 (trade paperback)
ISBN 978-1-250-33758-0 (hardcover)
ISBN 978-1-250-88267-7 (ebook)

Our books may be purchased in bulk for promotional, educational, or business use. Please contact your local bookseller or the Macmillan Corporate and Premium Sales Department at 1-800-221-7945, extension 5442, or by email at MacmillanSpecialMarkets@macmillan.com.

First Edition: 2024

10 9 8 7 6 5 4 3 2

To Abigail. You made me a mom.
Best first pancake ever.

CONTENTS

Momma
CUSSES

FOREWORD

You're about to read a book my mom wrote. First, I'm really proud of her. Second, I'm really glad this book is in your hands because it means she's done writing it and she probably hasn't made me read any of it in a long time. Actually, probably not, as I know full well she is just gonna move on to another book. So like . . . wish me luck, I guess. Anyway, my mom and I thought it would be sort of cool to have a foreword written by the child mentioned a lot in the book that follows. So somehow I got homework for her book. Cool.

I'm the Abbi she talks about. I'm the first pancake.

The firstborn child is like the first pancake: It's always kinda messed up.

I'm the one who got both the reactive parenting and the responsive parenting you're going to read about. (My mom gave me those terms. I don't talk like that. I don't think anyone but my mom talks like that.) And I wanted to let you know that it's okay. It's okay if you yelled a lot. It's okay if you didn't have it all figured out. It's okay if you feel liked you messed up. You might have. And that's still okay. My mom and I figured out how to be close and to talk and to listen better even though she used to yell and spank and do things that I know she kinda regrets. She said sorry and we sort of moved on from there. It wasn't immediate and it took some time and working through trust issues for us both. You'll get there too. Maybe my mom's book will help. Maybe it won't. But you're still okay.

—Abbi Laithland

FIELD GUIDE INSTRUCTIONS AND USAGE NOTES

What follows is a book. You're welcome for that helpful information.

More specifically, what follows is NOT a "fix-all" parenting handbook. It's not a bible. It's not the world's most perfect guide to raising the most perfect children. It's a collection of ideas that might be good. They might work for you. They might not. And that's . . . okay.

Each chapter covers some of the biggest, baddest, scariest aspects of parenting intentionally and responsively.

So here's how this book is going to work. Each chapter is focused on one particular concept you might find useful in figuring out how to raise your tiny human. Dotted through the book are little situation-specific entries you'll find useful. These are like survival guide hot tips; field guide entries. They are more focused on a particular challenge or issue we face as we attempt to parent intentionally, or responsively.

FIELD GUIDE ENTRY: *Kid Nicknames*

Names have power. It's why, as parents, we spend an inordinate amount of time trying to find a name for our children. We argue and worry. The name we give our child is the first thing that moves them from idea to actual, living person. Most pregnant people find calling their in-utero offspring "it" kind of uncomfortable. So we either find out the gender or we give it a nickname. Blueberry, Pinto Bean, Pumpkin Seed. Shortly after that we settle on a name and have whole conversations with the being we are growing with our bodies (or our partners are growing with theirs).

We spend a ton of mental energy and time finding a name to call our children to then immediately develop nicknames for them. Bubba, Tater Tot, or some weird abbreviation of the name we wrote on their birth certificates. The further into parenting we get, the weirder those nicknames get. I routinely refer to children, both mine and others', by a host of interesting nicknames. This is true in real life and in this book.

My pet names and nicknames reflect my "uses humor as a coping mechanism" personality trait. For ease of reference and by popular demand, I present a wildly incomplete list of things I've referred to children as in this book, in my social media work, and to my children's actual faces.

    Womb Fruit
    Chaos Goblin
    Crotch Goblin
    Sex Trophy
    Microscopic Swim Meet Champion
    Rage Demon
    Tiny Human
    Beta-Version Human
    Practice Person

Icicle Licker

Evicted Parasite

Small Human

Spawn

Spider Spawn

Ankle Biter

Flesh-Wrapped Potato

Sentient Meatloaf

This manual was crafted by an elder millennial who has spent a potentially embarrassing amount of time in internet spaces. As a result, some of the language and vernacular is very . . . internetty. Like that word. Real people do not use words like "internetty," except elder millennials who have spent too much time on said internet. Terms like "unalive" (to die, kill, or be dead) or "fee-fees" (feelings), using "person" as a verb, and other chaotic abuses of the general structure and grammar of the English language will occur throughout. If you're ever in doubt about the use of a word, roll with it. You can hit up the internet if you're really, really brave, ask your nearest millennial friend, or just use context clues. The author would like to apologize but it is very likely she would be unable to do so without the weird phraseology.

Warning before reading further: If brown is your favorite color in the world, there are needlessly lengthy portions of this book wherein the author brutally lambasts the color. She makes it clear she does not like the color and is obviously using this platform to make it known unto the world. The author's distaste for the color brown is her own strongly held and verbosely expressed opinion and should not be viewed as anything other than that. It's okay if you like brown. Yes, it should be noted that this is a field guide to parenting, not color theory, and it is not readily apparent how the color brown plays into parenting philosophy. At no point will that be made clear so be prepared to just live with that.

ADDITIONAL NOTES

The author does think she is funny. As a result, she tries entirely too hard sometimes. As evidenced by this entire paragraph. Prepare yourself. She does use and abuse puns from time to time.

At the end of each chapter appears a "too long; didn't read" summary. Labeled as "TL;DR," this will provide a hopefully partially useful summary of the chapter. Probably. The information will be incomplete but that's because hopefully you actually read the chapter and are not relying solely on TL;DR summaries to help you grasp the content of the book you bought or borrowed. If this book is stolen, well . . . that's bad. But at least you're reading it. Clearly you've got some feelings you need to work through and information in this book might be useful in doing so.

INTRODUCTIONS AND WHAT-NOTS

Hello. My name is Gwenna Laithland and I am not a parenting expert. I am, like, 98 percent sure that is not how the author of a parenting book is supposed to open said parenting book. However, I'm not a writing expert either so this feels like the move here. Truthfully, I have chosen to open a book on parenting by clearly stating that I'm not a parenting expert because I need to set the tone for what you're about to read. That feels important.

Let's get this bit out of the way. There is no such thing as a parenting expert. No one knows better how to raise a kid than anyone else. There are some people with good ideas. (I'd like to hope I'm one of those good-idea folks.) Some of those ideas will work for some but fail miserably for you. It doesn't make them bad ideas, just makes them bad for you. And that's okay.

I do believe there are experts in some fields that sort of hover around parenting. There are absolutely experts in child development norms. Behavioral therapists, childhood psychologists, child development researchers—they know their stuff surrounding some very specific elements of child development and standards of behavior. They also speak in generalities. They work in averages and norms. If a child is falling below the average, it is their job to ascertain why and provide assistance, guidance, and tools to bring that kiddo back up to normal.

That doesn't make them parenting experts.

Pediatricians, pediatric specialists, childhood nutritionists—these are also folks who have an absurd amount of knowledge about a very specific part of how kids are, how they should be, and what to do if said kids are encountering struggles of the physiological variety.

That doesn't make them parenting experts.

It makes them uniquely equipped to give advice to the only known parenting expert on any particular kid—their actual parent. Yep, if a parenting expert were to exist, you'd be one. You're an expert on your child. And if you react to this revelation the way I did when it first occurred to me, you now understand why I say there's no such thing as parenting experts. I'm most definitely not an expert. Even on my own kids. That I made. With my body.

I, like you, am simply doing my best.

Oh. You're still here? You got through that preachy part and are like, yes, Gwenna, give me more?

Alright.

Let's do this then.

This book is not a memoir. And, as I made abundantly clear several paragraphs ago, I'm not a parenting expert. But in order to understand how I've come to some of the conclusions I'm about to describe, it's important you know how I got here, who the hell decided to publish a book I wrote, and why any of it might be useful to you.

THE BACKSTORY

The United States Air Force was an awfully dull place in the 1980s. Vietnam was kind of fresh in the collective memory but it was a fading entity as far as the armed forces were concerned. Also, it was the air force. Not the *Top Gun* type. The pencil-pushing, makers-of-red-tape type. My mom was in facilities planning. For a brief period in the late eighties to nineties, Tinker Air Force Base was absolutely drenched in a putrid taupe, burnt orange, and cream color scheme. That was literally my mom's fault. She picked those colors as part of her super-important, patriotic duty–upholding, serving-the-country job in the air force. For those of you who lived on or near Tinker during this period, she is sorry.

My mom, by her own admission, joined the military because she couldn't think of anything better to do. She was socially awkward and insecure but she was detail-oriented, levelheaded, and low-maintenance. She had a slow-burning wit. She'd say something and you wouldn't even register how funny she was until moments later, once you'd had a chance to take a good swig of your beverage. There were a lot of spit takes around my mom as a result. It was one such spit take that helped her pull my dad.

My dad was an overgrown toddler with the emotional capacity of balsa wood who was strangely good with wrenches. He was a mechanic who worked on the AWACs, the big radar planes with the black domes perched on top of the body. Since those were peak technology at the time, it meant that my dad was an overgrown toddler with a really high security clearance. He did not have a slow-burn wit. His was loud and obvious and rakishly devastating. Look, Imma make it awkward for a sec, but my dad, in his heyday, was fucking hot. And he knew it. I'm talking Tom Selleck didn't stand a chance. And if you understood that reference, hi, Mom.

They met through a friend of a friend, and instantly created their own maelstrom of emotional chaos. It wasn't just sparks. It was Tesla coil meets Faraday cage with enough electricity coursing through their twenty-something souls to black out the Eastern Seaboard. They fell in love with the idea of each other. Unfortunately, they sort of had the wrong ideas in their heads. More on that later.

They married in 1980, got stationed at Tinker the same year. I was born in 1984. My mom left the military to be my mom. My dad stayed in. Mostly because being funny and turning wrenches were kind of all he was good at. They brought me home to their fifties-built, two-bedroom house but not before covering every square inch of it in the drab, earthy tones of mud, old coffee grounds, and cockroach wings. Really, my parents were sort of ahead of their time, readily embracing the tiny-home life and the preternatural appreciation for shades of sepia.

Hazelnut carpet, faux-wood wall paneling, coffee-stain paint, burnt sienna Formica countertops. Umber, ochre, beige. Everywhere. It was suffocating. The only room that escaped the tawny tidal wave was my room. They painted that one a baby blue. Even though I was a girl. And they knew that before I arrived. I once asked my mom why my nursery turned childhood bedroom turned teenage angst den was blue instead of pink and she explained that one time she read an article that said blue made babies calm and pink made them hyper, so she painted my room blue.

"Did it make me a calm baby?" I asked.

"No. You had anxiety," she replied nonchalantly. In that brief conversation I learned two things. Parents have been swinging for the fences and missing for generations and I was just born anxious. Cool.

It is important to note that not only was I born anxious, I was born deaf. Not profoundly, just deaf enough to not hear words and sound distinction properly. My mom was understandably concerned. (Because moms have felt an unnecessary amount of pressure involving infant and toddler milestones since the dawn of time.) She took me to our family doctor on the air force base, a stoic officer clearly biding his time until his retirement from the United States Air Force medical machine. According to my mom, he spent about six minutes with me, asked me to repeat a few words, showed me a few pictures of fruit, and then confidently declared I was clearly exceptionally delayed. Except he didn't say "exceptionally delayed." He used the *R* slur. The military healthcare system of the eighties was actually terrible at pretty much everything.

My mother was having none of it. She sought a second, civilian opinion. That doctor examined me thoroughly and easily decided I was not exceptionally delayed. I just couldn't hear anything. A quick surgery, a set of tubes, and intense speech therapy, and I was as caught up as could be. It was the first time my mom advocated for me. It would not be the last time. But again, this book isn't about me.

Due to the nature of what he did for a living and that he did that for the US military, my dad spent more of my childhood abroad than he did at home. Constant temporary duty assignments (TDYs) and quick trips to Alaska or Japan or Germany to work on a plane were the rhythm of my earliest years. My dad once sent me Kool-Aid from Egypt while on a temporary duty assignment. He spent a lot of time over there in Egypt and Saudi Arabia. Note of interest: Egyptian Kool-Aid either (1) doesn't taste any different than American Kool-Aid, or (2) does not exist because my dad just bought plain ol' regular Kool-Aid at the base exchange. The latter is most likely. I still thought it was cool because it came from Egypt. And Egyptian stuff was cool.

My life continued in the traditional suburban way until 1992 when my parents realized two very important things. First, my dad was not one with the big brain thoughts. Instead he was the kind of stand-up guy who brings a girlfriend home while his wife is halfway across the country at her sister's funeral. The kind of dude who expects his mouthy eight-year-old to keep that mouth shut about Daddy's special friend. My dad was an absolute shoebox who wildly overestimated the secret-keeping abilities of an undiagnosed ADHD kid. Second, they actually despised one another. They wanted to be married. Just not to each other. And yeah, that led to divorce.

Advanced for my age and in one of the first generations of academically advanced students referred to as "gifted and talented" kids, I entered my angst stage younger than many. Upon learning about my parents' divorce, I skipped the preteen exploration and dove straight into my weepy period. There was a lot of the color black. There was even more really bad poetry. Luckily for all of us, I also enjoyed a pyromaniac stage and destroyed the evidence.

A lot of that poetry, written primarily in red ink, focused on my being a statistic. Divorce was still pretty demonized in

Oklahoma in the mid-nineties. Our state often made national news for having one of the highest divorce rates. I did not enjoy my two Christmases and two birthdays. I would have settled for one if I didn't have to deal with custody exchanges. I would have settled for next to nothing if it meant I didn't have to endure a stepmom.

The girlfriend my dad brought home eventually became my stepmom. We hated each other. That's not an exaggeration. The resentment was very real from both sides. To me, she was a home-wrecker and an invader (although I'd later learn those titles really belonged to my dad). To her I was the usurper and liability. We screamed at each other. My dad gifted me his genetic proclivity to humor. I honed those sarcastic genes to a razor's edge at my stepmother's expense. The relationship was beautifully complicated.

And then it wasn't. One May afternoon in 1996, I sat out on my porch waiting for my dad to pull up in his ghastly blue Pontiac for a visitation exchange. He never showed up. I waited until the sun sank below the horizon before moving inside and waiting some more. This was in the days before cell phones, but we did have a house phone. Ours never rang. I tried to call him. All it did was ring. Years later I'd find out he didn't die in some fiery crash. Instead he let his little girl die a slow death by attrition on a porch barely warmed by Oklahoma's spring sun. What was left behind was someone new.

Thus I was created as I am now: an anxious, hard of hearing, intelligent to a fault, dangerously witty and trained in its weaponization, burnt-out gifted and talented kid with daddy issues who still finds herself wondering about Egyptian Kool-Aid sometimes.

My mom raised me the best way she could with the tools

she had available. I asked her once if she found being a single mom harder than being a not-single mom.

"Just because I was married to your father doesn't mean I wasn't always a single mom," she said more than once.

Told you she has a slow burn to her wit.

My mom was never a responsive parent. First, that term didn't exist and wouldn't until at least the later half of the 2010s. Second, she never had the time to consider more than a split-second reaction. In her years married to an enlisted man, nothing was predictable. Raising an infant, the whims of the military, convincing miles of red-tape-wrapped military medical drones that her child was not mentally exceptional, chasing the Oscar for acting like her husband definitely wasn't sleeping around—those things didn't leave a lot of time for introspection and refining one's parenting technique.

After the divorce, there was dealing with being imminently unqualified for anything not involving taupe paint, going to college, finding a job, and keeping us from calling the back seat of the teal Chevrolet Cavalier home, which took up just as much time. In the wake of her dissolved relationship with my dad, she swore off dating. That was the most responsive decision she made when I was a child. Again, please don't read that as finger-pointing or blame. She was doing her goddamned best and I will always be grateful for every reaction she settled on.

Here's where I sound contradictory. Her most carefully considered parenting choice—the decision not to date after divorce, focusing instead on her role as provider, guardian, and mother—really bit me in the ass. I ended up with zero frames of reference for how to relationship. I understand why and how she made that choice, both for her sake and mine. At least I would come to understand that.

When I got to adulthood, I was rather unprepared for coupling. And by rather unprepared I really mean completely devoid of anything resembling knowledge of how to maintain a relationship. Now because I went to public school, dating and relationships were not the only things I was dreadfully unprepared for. But those turned out to be especially problematic.

All that gifted-and-talented cred did get me into a kick-ass college. I got a full scholarship at my first pick of schools, a private Methodist university no one has ever heard of. It was an elite affair that I completely squandered. After dating the weirdest guys I could find, I settled on a high school dropout with a criminal record who lived with his mother and smoked two packs of Camels a day. I threw away my scholarship because he completed me like no degree ever could.

We got married. I wore a white dress. He burnt a hole in his rented tux with a joint. We said "I do" in front of seven people. None of them were our dads. Daddy issues have a way of really connecting twentysomethings. The knot was tied in November. I was pregnant by the New Year. He was furious. I was terrified.

I didn't know it then, but our marriage was over before it began. Just like my parents had been, I was in love with the idea of love. I wanted what I knew my mother missed. I wanted to collect that experience of feeling wanted. I confused my ownership of a vagina and a willingness to have sex with losers with the sensation of being loved.

I did get my wish though. I did figure out what love was. It still involved my vagina, weirdly. My eldest daughter, Abigail, was born in October 2007 when I was twenty-three, and a billion tiny little pieces fell into place for a fraction of a second. When they handed her to me the universe gifted unto me a nanosecond of true, unadulterated clarity of what it was to love another human being. Then she wiggled and something gooey touched me. I lost that newfound understanding as that perfect lucid moment shattered because birth, generally speaking, is gross and newborns come out kinda slimy. It would take me six more years, a divorce, a dating spree, a second marriage, and the imminent threat of more children to put all those pieces back together again. Those stories are elsewhere in this book.

THE CURRENT STORY

I ended up divorcing my eldest's father in 2010 and took a couple of years to do the very cliché "finding myself." To be fair, I had no idea who I was. Twenty-three is a weird age. It gets weirder when you have a baby at that age. I did decide to date again in 2012. I met Jackson Laithland in July of that same year. Our story is one for another time, but I'll give you the CliffsNotes. We met on the internet. We fell in love over quotes from *The Hitchhiker's Guide to the Galaxy* and a mutual appreciation for red Speedos. (No. I will not elaborate on that. Just take it for what it is.) We got married in 2014 and Jackson heartily and happily took on the mantle of father figure for Abigail. We decided quickly to expand our family and have a baby together. My uterus thought it was a funny joke and took four years to take my demand to be impregnated again seriously.

Ultimately, I did get knocked up, this time with twins. A boy and a girl. They were born in 2018. Since day care was prohibitively expensive, especially for two infants at the same time, I left the traditional workforce and became a stay-at-home mom. I also learned that I really sucked at being a stay-at-home mom. The repetition, the constant touching, the default parent status. It's hard. It kind of sucks. And, to be honest, once we got out of the godforsaken infant stage, it was kinda boring but in a stressful, I-can't-stop-moving, I'm-permanently-exhausted kind of way.

In order to break up the monotony, I turned to the internet, specifically TikTok. As it turns out, how I view my children, my role and work as a mom, and the decisions I was making about how to both keep them alive and help them learn how not to be assholes turned out to be kinda relatable. And if you're reading this because you follow me on some platform, somewhere on the internet . . . hi. I love you too.

I posted a few videos about how narrowly I was clinging to my sense of self as a mother. People responded. Then the world shut down in a global pandemic. I kept making videos. People kept responding. And then they started asking me questions. And I started trying to answer them. But in a very "me" way. Which includes mind-boggling ways to use words, and funny, borderline disrespectful nicknames for one's offspring like "womb fruit" and "beta-version humans."

I began to realize it wasn't just information folks were seeking online, especially since, again, this was happening in 2020 when we had to celebrate birthdays over Zoom and visit grandparents in literal bubbles in an effort to stave off the spread of COVID-19. People wanted connection. They wanted to feel not alone. And parenting can be very, very isolating. Hearing from another mom that looked like them (kinda—my hair is always vibrant, sometimes jarring colors) and sounded like them (potty-mouthed and perpetually tired) lay claim to the same struggles, complaints, confusion, and frustrations felt nice. It felt like maybe they weren't bad people for not wanting to play Candyland or for having envisioned the detailed demise of certain children's toy designers. I realized I had an opportunity to normalize modern parenting, and for reasons I'm still fucking confused about I was gaining a platform to do it.

And here we are. Me writing a book on parenting despite not being a parenting expert, lacking any formal accreditation or alphabet soup, and you reading it hoping I stop talking about myself and get to the shit you actually need, like how not to fuck up your kid. I'm making no promises on that last bit. Moving on.

One last thing: throughout the book, I share stories about my children. Because it's a book about parenting, and stories of parenting my children are kind of a big chunk of a book on parenting. However, it feels important to slap a disclaimer on some things. Many times I am nonspecific about which child I am referring to. That's a little bit on purpose. I've spent quite a bit of time existing on internet spaces and there is no shortage of discourse about children's digital footprints, online autonomy, and the line between parenting discussion and child exploitation. Writing a book on parenting is no different. I've changed some details to protect my children. No middle schooler wants to walk into class and be greeted with "I read your mom's book. Did you really [insert embarrassing story their mom overshared]?" So, while the stories are true and a part of my lived experience as a parent, it's not always going to be clear which child blessed me with that experience, lesson, or shareable moment. If that feels confusing or frustrating, I totally understand. But you get where I'm coming from, right?

And while we are disclaimering things, I occasionally share stories of others in my family. Again, some names and small details have been changed to protect the privacy and identity of those described.

And that's it. That's my childhood and the advent of a mom. It's how you ended up with a book about it in your hands. Now that you've got the backstory, let's press on, shall we?

TOO LONG; DIDN'T READ (TL;DR)

There's no such thing as a parenting expert. Except you. You're the expert on raising your own kid. Gwenna was not parented responsively but isn't mad about it. Her dad wasn't very bright. Her mom was trying her best. This is a book about parenting. Gwenna uses weird words a lot. She is not sorry.

EXPLANATIONS AND WHY-NOTS

Yes. Traditionally you go from chapter to chapter in whole numbers. But in this case what I'm about to share isn't really its own chapter. It also isn't really attached to the one before or the one after. So you get this. At least you are learning what you signed up for by picking up this book pretty early on. It makes no sense. Kinda like parenthood.

So you've got the vaguest notion that I'm not a parenting expert. No alphabet soup after my name. No credentials to speak of beyond "in the trenches" parenting. Why, then, should you give a damn what I say in this book about parenting? If I'm being brutally honest, and most of the time I am, it's because I have a way with words, I've probably felt what you've felt, and I'm a normal person who has come out the other end with a healthy amount of perspective on how not to feel like you're doing a shit job by your kids.

There are hundreds of excellent parenting writers I look up to and admire, not just as writers of parenting books but as humans and people. Writers like Carla Naumburg, Michaeleen Doucleff, Melinda Wenner Moyer, Emily Oster. They have their shit together as far as writers of books go. And if their bodies of work and professional credentials have anything to add, they are amazing women and mothers. Science, world travel, sociology, psychology, economics, mathematics. These writers used their extensive life experience, academic prowess, and professional connections to craft some of the seminal works I routinely reference when I hit my own parenting conundrums. Until the release of this book you're reading, if you'd asked me for a book recommendation, my go-to answer would have been Carla's *How to Stop Losing Your Sh*t with Your Kids*. Really. It feels real bold of me to try to hang with them, to put forward my book on parenting and have even half a hope of keeping up. I'm just some middle-aged mom with a social media following who accidentally hit it big on TikTok.

Wow, Gwenna, you're really selling yourself here. Keep going. I definitely don't want to put this book down and go find those other books. Nope, not the effect you're having at all.

Okay, yeah, I get that. But if you look really hard, my lack of all the expertise and formal education means that what I have to offer is no more or less than what you need. Chances are damn high this is not the first parenting book you've ever read or attempted to read. If you have chosen to read this book *because* you follow me on TikTok or Instagram or YouTube, there's a not-zero percent chance you have read Carla or Melinda or Emily already. But you're still reading parenting books because you still have questions they haven't been able to answer. And often for every answer you do get when asking yourself, how do I not be the reason for my kids' therapy?, you end up with sixteen more questions. So you keep reading

books and blogs and articles while listening to parenting pod-
casts and watching TikToks and YouTubes.

In some instances a parenting writer or creator's best effort
didn't help you understand. It directly addressed the parenting
issue you're trying to puzzle out. But it didn't actually help you.
So you had to keep digging. The solution they suggested was
all fine and dandy but there is no way in hell you can find time
in your day to practice meditative yoga. You have no doubt
that would help you cool your jets and be a little less reactive
with your kids, but that's not gonna happen. It's a solution,
sure. But not a good solution for you.

I make a habit of using two important statements in my
videos and productions.

1. Will this work for every family? No. But it works for
   ours.
2. If an idea doesn't work for you or your family, it
   doesn't make it a bad idea. It makes it a bad idea for
   you.

Hence, I'm writing a parenting book. Because my uncre-
dentialed, learned primarily by trial and error, still feeling like
I'm making it up as I go parenting style might be the good idea
that works for you. What works for my family might never,
ever fly in Melinda Wenner Moyer's household, but it just
might scratch the itch you haven't been able to reach in your
own home.

So yeah, I'm adding a book to my repertoire of online content. I'm not expecting it to revolutionize parenting on the
whole. For so many reasons, no single book is going to. And
I'm not trying to top or outdo those writers and creators who

have come before. I'm simply adding my perspective and experience to the catalogue, just in case someone has that lightbulb moment because of how I approached, explained, or viewed a parenting issue. Will everything in this book work for you? God, I hope so. But in case it doesn't, that's okay. My feelings aren't hurt.

Okay, that's enough weird humblebrags. Now on to the next full-length chapter.

TL;DR

This book exists because Gwenna's unique way of viewing parenting and explaining it might help people wrap their heads around the ginormity of parenting responsively. Many parenting authors have come before and many will come after. But that doesn't mean there isn't space for this book on the shelves or in your head.

· 2 ·

WHY I HATE GENTLE PARENTING

Okay, I don't actually hate gentle parenting. But after years of having to write clickbait headlines to get people to give me more than two seconds of their attention, old habits die hard. If pressed, I'd have to admit that I actually find myself drawn to the ideas of gentle parenting. What are those ideas?

That isn't an easy question to answer. A lot of people have a lot of different ways to define it. Ask a parent elbow deep in Montessori-based parenting methods and their answer is going to look a lot different than a parent who adheres to a free-range parenting ideology.

Here's how I understand and break down gentle parenting:

1. **Prioritizing the emotional development of your tiny human with care and functional tasks.** As humans, we are born not knowing most of the things humans do. As parents, it is generally our job to provide for our

children's needs and teach them all the stuff they don't know. (So, everything.) For the gentle parent, teaching kids what they are feeling, that those feelings are okay, and healthy ways to handle those feelings is as important as learning not to poop in your pants or how to use a fork.

Example: Learning how to tie your shoes is hard. Teaching a tiny human with questionable fine motor skills and the attention span of, well . . . a child, is arguably harder. It is frustrating for everyone and there are points, several of them, in the process where you both think, is it really that big a deal if we just wear Velcro and slip-on shoes for the rest of our lives? That feels maybe better than learning bunny ears and trees and swoops and pulls. For a gentle parent, it is important to acknowledge that frustration that everyone is feeling. And it's okay if they don't have it down quickly. Give the time that is needed rather than what is expected. You can let you and your kid be frustrated without letting either of you give up.

2. **Setting, enforcing, and reevaluating boundaries.** Humans need boundaries. We need them for both our safety and our sanity. Some boundaries aren't easily or often crossed. Most of us (though apparently not all of us, given the popularity of true-crime documentaries) know not to kill people. Driving the speed limit? A lot of us test that boundary more often than we probably should. Kids need the same. Gentle parenting is not permissive parenting. Boundaries are one of the most vital parts of teaching kids how to exist without us.

Setting and enforcing boundaries is the framework we create to teach our children both self-control and respect or empathy for others.

Example: In our home we have precious few no-go zones. Mom and Dad's closet is only off-limits at Christmastime because that's where we hide the presents. And the kitchen is a no-no but only when Mom is cooking because we don't want melted babies and broken ankles. The littles aren't allowed in the eldest's room unless she has specifically invited them inside. Beyond that, we all get to exist in the space we require, wherever that may be. So when I bought and set up a fancy little desk in the corner of our living room and announced that no one, even Dad, was allowed to be at my desk without express and written permission, it was a bit of a boundary puzzle. We had never had a "No touching" sign on anything in the common areas. That which was not allowed was locked up, out of sight, out of mind. But this big ol' desk with a fancy computer and lots of clickable buttons and keys was off-limits. The audacity my kids must have assumed I had. But the boundary was important. And we reminded the kids of this often, sometimes loudly. Eventually the novelty wore off, the boundary became clear and clearly immovable, and they started ignoring the desk and everything on it. My computer (and the important projects on it) were protected, not by locks and keys and baby gates but by boundaries.

3. **Enforcing natural and actionable consequences.** When a boundary is crossed, there is a consequence. Adults understand this dynamic. Kids don't know shit, so it

is our job as parents to teach this principle. Gentle parenting prefers natural consequences when possible or safe. Natural consequences, summed up, are: If you jump off the roof aiming for the trampoline, you'll hurt yourself. That's the punishment. You yeeted yourself down fifteen feet and now you have an owie—probably a bad one. If the natural consequence would result in loss of blood, limb, or life, (like throwing oneself off a roof), the gentle parent instead chooses an actionable consequence that fits the boundary crossed. You can't let them play on the roof, so the actionable consequence hopefully dissuades them from climbing up there in the first place. Since you are using the trampoline to get up on the roof and make unsafe choices, I'm taking the trampoline springs away.

Example: My daughter got her first tablet at the age of ten. If you're thinking, wow, mine got it at ten months, no worries. I'm not judging. My littles got tablets at two. But tablets were much more expensive and we were much more broke when my oldest child was little. She got it for Christmas one year and she was obsessed. She downloaded this fish game that involved swimming around the ocean eating fish smaller than you and avoiding sharks. The tablet lasted approximately three months before she raged at the machine and snapped it on her knee because she kept getting eaten by the same shark on the same level. She took another three months to tell us she had broken the tablet. When she finally fessed up she asked if we were going to fix it.

I told her, "Absolutely not. You got the tablet. You didn't care for the tablet. You don't got the tablet."

Then she tried to use my own gentle parenting against me: "But I was mad. You're telling me I'm wrong for being mad?"

Clever girl. I replied, "You're not wrong for being mad. You're wrong for making it my problem. You got mad and instead of taking a step back and a break from the game, you tried to press ahead, this time angry. It resulted in you losing both your temper and your control. You broke the tablet and now want me to get it fixed. Nope. I gave you tools to handle your anger before it got out of hand. Since you weren't able to do that, you have a broken tablet to show for that. That's the natural consequence you've got to deal with."

If she'd had another tablet on hand she might have broken that one too. Ultimately she did get a new tablet several months after that conversation for her birthday, this time with a thick gummy case on it and strict instructions to never, ever download the shark game. She did not download the game. And she didn't break another tablet out of rage either. The natural consequence stuck that time.

4. **Teaching and granting autonomy.** At its very core, gentle parenting is the recognition that our job as parents is not to create good kids, but to help them evolve into happy, healthy, stable adults. This begins with respecting our kids as people. Tiny people hell-bent on accidentally unaliving themselves in admittedly creative ways at times, but people nonetheless. Gentle parents

give their children as much autonomy or ability to make their own decisions as often as is safe (and convenient). Gentle parents also acknowledge autonomy through explanations when appropriate and apologies when necessary.

Example: The year I began writing this book was the year I abandoned bedtimes for the eldest. She had turned fifteen and I told her I no longer cared when she went to bed as long as (1) she stayed in her room after 10 p.m.; (2) I could not hear what she chose to do with her late-night time; and (3) I did not see her schoolwork slipping or get calls or notes that she was falling asleep in class. I granted her the autonomy to decide when to go to sleep while she was still living with me because if she started making poor choices in regard to her sleep schedule, I still had an opportunity to help her correct that. It's been just under a year now and we have not seen much in the way of negative consequences for her autonomy. Unless you count taking more naps. But I think that's just how teenagers work, bedtimes notwithstanding.

On the whole, I've found that most people fundamentally misunderstand gentle parenting. They get really hung up on the word "gentle." It feels too nice. Especially to parents already in the thick of it. Parents who have fought the good fight, say, of convincing an eight-year-old that he isn't Spider-Man and that hanging from the ceiling in the hallway is less than ideal, look at "gentle" and it feels absurd.

For folks whose love language is sarcasm or those who

would say "fuck" is among their favorite words, the term "gentle" also feels out of place. It almost feels like in order to be a gentle parent, you have to be a gentle person.

Once upon a time, I was one of those people. I didn't start intentionally parenting my oldest child until she was around six or seven. The Mom Shame (notice I called it Mom Shame, not Mom Guilt; more on that in a later chapter) in me wants to say that's unfortunate. But the reality is, I was stuck in survival mode. I accidentally got pregnant sooner than anticipated. If you'd asked twenty-two-year-old Gwenna when she wanted to have kids, she would have answered "the seventeenth of never," so it was a lot sooner than anticipated. Shortly after my daughter was born, I found myself needing to escape an abusive partner, set up a home, learn to single mom, keep a job to pay all the bills, keep the kid alive, and somehow heal my emotional and physical traumas.

I was on autopilot. When faced with a parenting choice, I didn't so much make one as I defaulted to whatever my mom had done with me. Luckily my mom had also done her best with the resources she had. She didn't always make the right choice, but none of us do. If it wasn't something I could draw on my own childhood for, I'd hit up the internet and do whatever Reddit suggestion or Facebook moms' group thread felt doable. I was emotional, unpredictable, reactive, and doing my best. Some of my parenting choices were great. Some were less than stellar. None of them were what I would say were on purpose. I was flying by the seat of my pants and flailing in the wind, to mix metaphors. I was not intentionally parenting, instead making all my decisions on whims and whispers. I was going with my gut and couldn't shake this idea that my gut was getting shit wrong.

The shift happened one day when I was good and deep in my feels. I'd had a rough day at work, my ex was being extra ex-y, my PT Cruiser had snapped a timing belt for the second time, and I discovered the chicken I'd thawed for dinner had spoiled. Carless, dinnerless, and absolutely spent, my daughter did something that broke the camel's back. I don't even remember what it was. Which means it was likely innocuous and perfectly acceptable for a child to have done. I twisted off and yelled at her. And I mean the neighbors three doors down heard me at a conversational volume. I roared out all my frustration, expecting a second grader to shoulder the burdens of my adult problems. And in that moment, I regained full consciousness. I rejoined reality as my daughter flinched at the words pouring, full bore, out of my mouth. Her shoulders were hunched, her little face was pinched trying not to cry, and she was making herself small.

It broke me. It absolutely destroyed me. None of those problems were her problems. None of what was setting me off was her fault. Even whatever she'd done to trigger me didn't make her deserving of my breakdown. I was the adult. She was the kid. And here she was handling my shit better than I was.

That was not the first time I apologized to her. My mom had given me that basic tenet of parenting. It was the first time I apologized and really, truly meant it, however. That little breakdown sent me into a flurry of research, reading, and resource hunting on how to never, ever be whatever the hell I'd morphed into in that uncontrolled moment. I wasn't without access to research or the ability to sift through it. Though I stopped short of getting a fancy diploma, I had been a history major in college with an emphasis on research. My job at the time was education-oriented and I had ready access to all sorts of childhood development degree holders. I knew how to get the answers on how not to fuck up your kids.

I've been known to be a bit of an over-self-educator. When I get panicked, intrigued, or scared of something, my solution was, and still is, to hyper-fixate and learn everything I possibly can about it. Thanks, ADHD. (A diagnosis that I would not actually get until years after The Big Blow-up.) I found myself attracted to gentle parenting in idea if not name.

All that being true, and given that I do practice all of those principles of gentle parenting, why do I hate gentle parenting?

The word "gentle" is a nice word. It indicates that you aren't an angry parent. It's also wildly misleading. There are definitely parts of parenting that are gentle. Trying to get a freshly sleeping baby into their crib without waking them and restarting the damn cry, eat, doze, rock, sleep cycle for the eighth time is certainly gentle. Putting a diaper on a refuses-to-potty-train toddler while they show you what a crocodile looks like in a death roll, decidedly less gentle.

That's why, for the purposes of this field guide, we are going to frame those ideas I listed above as responsive parenting.

Cool, long-winded story, Gwenna. How is the word "responsive" any better than "gentle"?

Excellent question. Thank you for asking. In truth, "responsive" might not be any more descriptive or accurate than "gentle." It is, however, an opposite-ish word to "reactive." Every ounce of my parenting prior to The Big Blow-up was reactive. I didn't or couldn't spare the emotional energy to put much forethought into how I was raising my daughter. I would address things as they became problems or in need of addressing and not a moment before.

And again, I remind you: This isn't a parenting book. It's

a field guide based on my parenting experience. I began parenting as a highly reactive mom, guessing and swinging for the fences, flying off the handle, and feeling generally lost and confused. I shifted to a more intentional, responsive mode of child-rearing, keeping in mind that I wasn't raising a child, I was raising a human who was gonna need to have her shit together at some point. Rather than instinctually or intuitively react to whatever parenting thing ended up in my lap, I tried to be intentional and metered in my responses. Hence, responsive parenting.

Ultimately, you get to call it whatever you want. Again, you're the best expert on your own kid and your own parenting style. (Just so we're clear, I'm going to remind you of this at least forty-three more times before our time together is up. It's important. And the sooner you believe that, the easier it will be to become the kind of parent you want to be.)

FIELD GUIDE ENTRY: *A Note for Fresh Parents*

If you are reading this and you are a fresh parent, meaning this is your first kid (or crop of kids in the case of multiples) and you still count your kid's age in months, I need you to know that much of what follows may not necessarily apply to you for a bit. As far as responsive parenting goes, there really isn't a whole lot to be done about the emotional development and autonomy of a child who still isn't 100 percent sure what their foot is.

The first year or so is nothing but survival for all parties. Your job is to make sure your sentient meatball of an infant is fed, clean, sheltered, and feels secure. It will do its damnedest to convince you none of those things are happening and definitely not in the correct order.

What I'm about to say will bring you comfort someday, but I doubt it will feel super useful if you are elbow deep in year one. Most of what your kid is going to learn in this first year of being human, they'll learn with or without your direct assistance.

Right now, you are likely deeply concerned about milestones, longing for the big firsts (smiles, laughs, words, foods, nights they just fucking sleep) and super focused on a very specific thing your kid isn't doing but you think maybe they ought to be doing by now. As you should. You're not wrong to worry about those things. Nothing I or anyone else can say will alleviate your worry about those things.

But a baby, given that its needs are being adequately met and it is provided a safe space to just exist, will figure most of that stuff out in its own time. Sure, tummy time helps strengthen core muscles and can make the rolling-over thing easier. But even if they never get tummy time, they'll roll over when they are good and ready to do so. Same with pulling up, crawling, pincher grab, vocalizations, babblecabulary, walking, and all the other fun stuff that happens the first year-ish. Kids do stuff in their own time, pediatrician milestones and toxic mom group humblebrags notwithstanding.

But Gwenna, what about...yes, I know. There does come a point at which it's time to ask the pediatrician why your kid isn't walking or if it's a problem that she doesn't really have many words. And I can't tell you what that point is. Best to ask. Your pediatrician, doctor, care specialist, whoever you trust with these sorts of analyses, would rather quell your fears a thousand times than miss a chance to get a child the extra assistance they need.

You know the phrase "You'll just know..."? I hate it. The deepest core of my ability to hate is founded upon hating the phrase "You'll just know..." I hate it that much because every time someone has told me "You'll just know....," they were fucking right. How will I know if I should marry this guy? When you're in love, you'll just know. How will I know if I'm actually in labor or if this is just another false contraction thingy? Oh, honey, when you're in labor, you'll know. How will I know if my kid needs early intervention or therapy of some sort? If your kid is struggling, you'll know. No, it's not universal. Yes, folks have missed the signs and not "just known." But if you are actively arguing with a book right now, you know. Go ask your healthcare provider about it. They can help better than I can.

FIELD GUIDE ENTRY:
A Note to Extra-Experienced Parents

Now we swing to the other end of kids-in-the-home parenting. If at least one of your kids has hit double digits or you will be moving a few of them out into the real world soon, you are an extra experienced parent. That's not to say you know what you're doing. None of us do. Not really. You've just made it this far. If you're that deep into the parenting gig, you've picked this book up for a reason. Maybe this is for confirmation that you aren't alone in what you're trying with your kids. Or maybe you aren't happy with where you are. You recognize your own reactivity and are looking for a way to change how you communicate and, by extension, the relationship you have with your not-so-tiny, tiny humans.

I want you to know, it is never too late to change course. You can shift your parenting technique at any point. If we want to get really specific, you've already done that at least a few times. You absolutely do not parent your school-ager the same way you parented them when they were toddlers. You shifted and adapted alongside them. The difference between those changes and an intentional swing in your parenting style is that this time, you'll notice.

Have you ever looked up at your kid and suddenly noticed how much they've changed? Like, all of a sudden, your once pudgy-bellied, bowlegged, pig-tail-sporting little girl is leaner, curvy in different places, and are those little baby booby sprouts under that T-shirt? One day you look at your son and notice his five-o'clock shadow. You know he's been shaving for a while now but the shift from baby face to stubble management happened slowly. Every day they change a little. But we are around them so much and the changes are so incredibly subtle, it's easy to miss the cumulative effects.

As if to twist the knife that is parenting ourselves out of a job, the universe will suddenly strike us with those harsh moments of awareness of just how much our children have grown. They've changed and we almost didn't notice. (And cue the Mom Shame, that wormy bitch.) We've been changing with them the whole time. As they gained new mastery of a skill or personality trait, we adapted how we communicate.

I have always been quick to joke and play with my kids. It's who I am as a person. Humor is my gift, my coping mechanism, and my defense mechanism. One of my favorite parts of my oldest continuing to get older is that she inherited my humor. I could never make the same type of irreverent jokes with the preschool version of my daughter. I adapted as my daughter grew. It wasn't really a choice, even after I shifted to responsive parenting. It's just the nature of growth.

So, you've already changed. Potentially several times. You can intentionally change this time. Somehow, the change you choose feels scarier than the ones that happened without your notice. I know. I've already been there. But it's not too late. Even if you're looking through college guides or are already breaking in your empty nest, any shift to being more aware of your communication, emotionally responsive, and receptive is going to result in a net positive.

You can't undo the mistakes that are currently gnawing on the fringes of your mind. You can't go back and change who you were then. You can only move forward. Responsive parenting can be a way to heal what feels hurt—both for you and your kids.

TL;DR

"Gentle" is the wrong word to describe this version or style of parenting. The word is too nice and gives the wrong impression. Gwenna is sick of explaining that. Basically, gentle parenting can be broken down into four important concepts:

1. Prioritizing the emotional development of your tiny human with care and functional tasks.
2. Setting, enforcing, and reevaluating boundaries.
3. Enforcing natural and actionable consequences.
4. Teaching and granting autonomy.

No matter what word you use, the concept remains the same. Gwenna prefers the term "responsive" because it feels like the opposite of "reactive."

· 3 ·

THE EASY PART

Yes, there is an easy part of parenting. The term "easy" is only used here as a comparative. No part of parenting is actually easy. But compared to the monumental task of ensuring your kids understand how to both use and protect the gray matter inside their skull and all the stuff the rest of this book covers, the care tasks and functional tasks are monstrously easier.

So, what are care tasks and functional tasks?

A **care task** is anything you do to meet your child's needs that they cannot, for whatever reason, do themselves. In the earliest days, that's everything. Think Maslow's Hierarchy of Needs: food, water, shelter. We provide all this and so much more for our womb fruit in their infancy. We make endless meals via boob, bottle, or meal prep. For a lot of the first year or more, we are responsible for physically inserting those meals into their bodies. We also clean up the aftermath of that via diaper changes.

Parents are responsible for teaching our crotch goblins literally everything. It doesn't help that human children are born
pretty much useless. Seriously, as far as complex organisms go,
human children are born painfully useless. Kangaroos, pan-
das, and people: all mammals who make weirdly vulnerable
offspring.

Horses, giraffes, and zebras are all walking within hours of
being born. Some species of fish and reptile ditch their young
the minute they exit their bodies. Can't develop daddy issues
if no one's got parents, I guess. Sharks are born straight-up
grown, just smaller. (Okay, maybe they aren't, but they are
pretty much independent from birth.)

Humans have huge, resource-hungry brains. Our bodies
use an extraordinary amount of our physical resources to keep
our gargantuan meat computers online. If a baby were to stay
in utero for much longer than the forty-ish weeks of human
pregnancy, the resource drain of keeping two bodies and two
brains alive could risk the continued existence of both. In es-
sence, our species is entirely too smart to produce anything
other than a mewling flesh-wrapped potato at birth.

That means, by default, parents have to do a lot of teaching. For the first year, a lot of skill learning is mildly automatic
as those big ol' baby brains straighten themselves out, figuring out what neurons should actually connect to each other
and pruning off the herky-jerky bits. They'll learn a certain
amount of muscle control which leads to gross and fine motor
skills (crawling, walking, grabbing stuff). Babies are naturally
inclined to be curious and to explore. (That's the nice way of
saying they are programmed from birth to get into shit.) After
that, it's on parents to kind of refine that base programming.

Cool, kid, you can definitely grab that charger wire and get it to your mouth. Now try that same motion with a spoon. Feed ya damn self. Thus, we arrive at a **functional task**. Anything a human is born not knowing how to do and later learns how to do is a functional task.

Pretty much all care tasks eventually become functional tasks. When we manage to get our kids potty trained, we've taken the care task of diaper changes and shifted it to the functional task of toilet hygiene. As the kid grows and gets better at handling their shit (heh-heh, puns and poop jokes. Highbrow stuff right here, folks), the less involved we are in the whole process. And unless there is a developmental delay, illness, or chronic condition in the mix, we aren't likely to be involved in the process of our kid voiding their bowels at all after a certain point.

The older our kids get the more complex the functional tasks become. We cook every meal for our kids, until we don't. Some of us get our kids in the kitchen early and they begin taking over some of their own meal or snack prep. Even for parents who decide sharp objects and hot surfaces are absolutely off-limits for younger humans (no judgment, I get it), once they move out, that becomes almost entirely their problem.

Our children begin their lives with a built-in chauffeur. Then they hit a magic age and are suddenly to be trusted with a ton or so of motorized sledgehammer. We'll set aside the fact that they haven't kept a phone screen intact for longer than two weeks and just hand them some car keys. Driving is a functional task that combines a whole bunch of other previously learned functional tasks. As with all things, eventually, the Mom Taxi Service shutters and the kid is hauling their own ass around.

Some functional tasks parents teach their own kids. Some they farm out to other members of the community. My mom knew damn well it wasn't in her to teach me how to drive. She gleefully signed me up for driving school when I came of age. When my daughter is old enough to drive, I'm also self-aware enough to nope myself out of that educational experience. Either my husband will teach her or she's going to driving school, just like her mom did.

Parents routinely find other folks to help them teach their kid the billion functional tasks humans have to learn. We send them to school to learn from trained educators how to read, write, and do some stuff with numbers. (I was less good at the numbers bit. But my teachers sure tried their hardest.) And that's just fine.

A parent's job isn't always to teach their kids. Sometimes it is to provide them opportunities to learn. Empowering others with a different set of resources to help your kid learn isn't a parenting fail. It's kind of baked into the cake of parenting. We simply cannot nor should be all things for our kids. We start out that way. First as incubator, if we are the uterus owner and producer of the child, and then as the doer of the care tasks. But ultimately, we are parenting ourselves out of a job.

And that's the easy part. Teaching or providing our children the chance to learn the accumulated knowledge of the entirety of human history. No big. No pressure. It's fine. Totally fine. Fuck.

I did warn you this part of parenting wasn't actually easy. I just think it's easier when compared to the next part. What's the next part? Excellent question. Thank you for asking.

Now begins *Momma Cusses*. Yeah, sorry, all that you just

read—technically still the introduction. But I figured if I called everything you've already read the introduction, you'd skip past it. I do. I never read intros. All that shit was important. Thanks for understanding. On we go.

TL;DR

Babies are born useless. We have to teach them to be not useless. We do this first through care tasks: doing stuff for our kids like feeding, bathing, time management. Then through functional tasks: teaching them how to do care tasks for themselves.

Sometimes we do this ourselves. Sometimes we can farm that teaching out to others like teachers, coaches, and tutors. Either way our kids learn how to be a person is fine.

· 4 ·

THE RISE OF EMOTIONALLY AWARE PARENTING

et's cover this again. Who is the parenting expert? You. You are the best expert on your child, your family, and your circumstances. Everything that follows are just good ideas (if I dare say so myself) that may or may not work for you. At the very least, they are ideas you can hold your own up to and confirm you still feel like your parenting method is working for you. Comparing notes, even if they don't say the same thing, is an excellent way to be intentional about the type of parent you are and how you raise your kids.

For a responsive parent, that lifetime of care and functional tasks is important. Equally important is helping our children accept, expect, and successfully embrace their own emotional states. Emotional development feels like a very fresh term to me. I can say for certain my emotional development was not on the radar back when I was growing up in the 1980s and

90s. Emotions just happened and you learned to deal with them. My mom, my teachers, my earliest mentors and employers had all come from the same school of thought.

"Figure it out, kid."
"Big boys and girls don't cry."
"Don't you look at me in that tone of voice."

If you're a Gen Z or millennial reading this, I probably just triggered you with at least one of those. Sorry. But those are familiar if not pleasant. Right or wrong, the idea of considering a person's mental health before it goes to shit really is kind of new-age thinking. Even the idea of having differing parenting styles feels new.

While working on this book I spoke to my mom often about how I was raised and how she came to the parenting decisions she came to. Partly because I hyper-fixate on stuff, and partly because my brain was technically always working on the book. And partly because a lot of what I was writing about was either in direct support or direct opposition to how I was raised. There is no middle ground.

My mom said that when I was born in 1984 there were precisely two books on parenting widely available. There might have been others but they weren't at the library closest her and she doesn't remember them. So if my mom needed child-rearing advice she could consult *What to Expect When You're Expecting, Dr. Spock's Baby and Child Care,* or the army (or air force if you wanna get technical) of other wives, mothers, and care providers in the neighborhood. Aaand that was it. If none of those shed any light on the situation, you just made shit up. Honestly that last bit feels familiar even with the whole of the internet at my fingertips. Good to see things haven't changed that much in the last thirty-plus years.

As I talked to my mom about various parenting styles and their names and traits, my mom was astounded. Helicopter, free-range, responsive, gentle, authoritarian—those words all made sense to her but she'd never have connected all of them to parenting.

My generation's mental health and emotional development wasn't really a huge factor in our youth. I mean, technically it was more or less our problem. I can't speak in absolutes. There have always been responsive, intentional, gentle parents. They might not have recognized their parenting by those terms but they existed nonetheless. And it could be argued that the children of the eighties and nineties had it better in terms of our emotional health than our parents in the sixties and seventies or grandparents of the forties and fifties.

Each generation has been granted a little more in the way of emotional guidance. As the topic of mental health got more attention and the stigma began to break down a bit more in the 2000s and 2010s, all those eighties and nineties babies were busy having babies of their own.

Voilà. A generation of adults given at least nominal access to information on mental health and emotional development is now in charge of the next generation. If you're reading this as a Gen X, millennial, Gen Z, or any generation betwixt those, congrats. You're the first groups of parents generally okay with getting yourself therapy. I'm unsure how I feel about knowing just how broken we are mentally. Like . . . great, we can assess and accept help. But also, damn. There's a shit ton of us with trauma. Mixed feelings. (But I can discuss those mixed feelings openly and without shame, so there's something there.)

So we are of an unprecedented mindset that it's okay to not be okay. And we are really working to undo the trite, diminishing concepts like "Hurt people hurt people." Hurt people can hurt people, but they can also acknowledge that they are more than their pain and use that pain to motivate themselves to do better. Yay, therapy!

Now we get to have better conversations about intentional parenting. And with the internet constantly available to connect us, shifting a mindset and trying new methods of raising not-shitty humans feels more doable than ever before. Our resource pool is infinitely bigger than our parents' or any generation's before them.

FIELD GUIDE ENTRY: *Generational Trauma*

It is at this juncture that I need to address the elephant in the room. Many folks who are either engaged in or considering a responsive parenting approach are here because they have no decent parenting role models to draw from. This might feel like a bold assumption about my readers, but I'm not stabbing in the dark. Hundreds of thousands of comments, DMs, and emails indicate that folks are actively seeking out ways to not raise their kids the way they were raised. Their own childhoods range from emotionally silent parents to downright traumatic and abusive experiences. A not-insignificant number of us are working not only on raising kids but reparenting ourselves. The only thing our parents provided for us was examples of what not to do.

So many—too many—responsive parents are opting for this intentional, emotionally available and aware style because they are breaking generational trauma. If that's you, hi! I see you. What you're doing is hard. It is valid. You are by no means alone in this attempt to be better than your parents, to do more for your kids than they did for you.

If any comfort is to be had about your struggle to not only heal what your childhood left broken, but to be the best parent you possibly can be to your own kids, it's this: None of us have any fucking clue what we are doing. Children with fairy-tale childhoods and supportive, available parents still very much feel like they are reinventing the parenting wheel with their own kids. Yes, they do have the privilege of having excellent examples when the standard trials of raising tiny humans arise. It helps to not have the only examples be the wrong examples.

But no two children are the same. And the children we are raising today have very different experiences. I was among the last to enjoy (or endure, whichever you choose) an analog childhood. All three of my children by contrast have known internet access and social media for the entirety of their existence. That means my mom provided zero reference material for how to decide when should my kid get a phone or how to talk about internet security and social media.

Each successive generation has encountered new, seemingly unprecedented struggles. Sure, some parenting problems are pretty universal. And some parenting questions have been asked for eons.

Being intentional about your parenting doesn't necessarily make parenting easier, no matter what sort of childhood references, education, or experiences you bring to the table. In some ways it makes it a wee bit harder because lashing out, while it will definitely happen because kids are assholes and parents are human, isn't allowed just because we are in a bad mood. Ultimately we want to be able to meter our own reactions to give our kids a good base for how to regulate their own feelings and moods.

This is, however, a bit of a double-edged sword. The internet is just ripe with really good creators, writers, psychologists, and childhood development professionals with all sorts of wonderful information to make us better, more informed parents. I mean ripe. Ripe-ripe. Overflowing. Abundant streams of information that are never-ending. It doesn't stop. There's so much information. Too much information. Some of it conflicts. Some of it is talking in circles. Did they just advocate for spanking by saying don't spank? Those are not the same thing. But apparently they are? And it's confusing. And overwhelming. And fuck it, I'm gonna doom-scroll Instagram 'cuz ugh.

The wealth of information just readily available at our fingertips can be a wonderful tool. It can also complicate things in nightmarish ways. Our language is imprecise on its best day. And when you filter it through written words that lack tonal indicators, or cram a really complicated issue into a bite-sized, sixty-second video, things can get muddy.

Take for example two chapters back where I swore off the word "gentle" in gentle parenting. I don't hate the word or the parenting style, but I'm really tired of explaining that gentle is not permissive. My kids are not going to grow up emotionally coddled just because I'm hoping to help them learn how to successfully navigate emotions. And that's a debate that rages on the internet. Based on one single word.

That's not to mention the diaper debates. The boob juice versus formula battleground. The absolute wasteland that is the anti-vaccination camp. While many of these debates are themselves as old as the things they argue about, they've really been given platform and volume by the internet.

I'm always very frightened for a person who shares with me

that they are expecting their first child. Not because parenting is hard, though that's true, but because I know that person is about to wade into the parenternet for the first time and it's terrifying in there. And that's not even addressing the minefields that are social media platforms. More on that in the next chapter.

There are so many voices of reason, experience, and wisdom. And they take into account the mental well-being of both parents and children. There's no one right way to raise a child. There's no one right way to be a parent. But when all that information is thrown at you at once, it's hard to sort out what feels right, what feels like something you want to give a go, and what just isn't a good fit. The TV personality has a good idea and the social media gal has a good idea but they directly conflict with each other in practice. How do you know which one to try?

In this case, we still find ourselves no better off than our parents or grandparents. We fucking guess. We take the spaghetti, chuck it at the wall, and see what sticks. Our advantage over our parents and grandparents is that our pot of spaghetti isn't quite as full. Each noodle was hand selected. We don't have a metric ton of noodles to sort through because with each generation, we've ruled some ideas out. We are pretty confident corporal punishment does bad things to tiny brains. Thus the corporal punishment noodle isn't in our proverbial pots. We get to hurl artisanal spaghetti at our aesthetically painted wall. It's better, even if just a little.

TL;DR

The act of parenting hasn't really changed over the course of history. But the amount of information we can exchange about *how* we parent definitely has. The more recent generations have been great about discussing and considering mental health and as a result we have created more resources about how not to mess up our kids emotionally. But this free flow of information can be a double-edged sword as there is such a thing as too much information. It can become confusing and overwhelming. Nevertheless it is still important to find a community of other parents to exchange ideas with, vent with, and get reassurance that you're doing okay. None of us have any idea what we are doing and that is okay.

· 4.5 ·

REPETITIVE REPETITION

Gwenna, we already had a chapter four. This is chapter five. You aren't very good at writing books.

You're right. On both counts. I have repeated chapter 4. I've repeated a few things, actually. You're five chapters in and I've told you at least three times that you are the best expert on parenting your own child. Maybe more, honestly, I'm too lazy to scroll back up and count. You'll find as you continue reading this book that I repeat concepts and ideas a lot. It's important. This is not an accident. This is by design and it serves a couple of different purposes.

Repetition is a part of parenting. Generally speaking it's a part of being human. We do a lot of repetitive tasks. Some folks love it. It's comforting, predictable, and routine. My husband adores mowing the lawn. I would rather sandpaper my own eyeball than make a single pass across the grass with the mower. Partly because I'm either the color of mayonnaise or the color of lobster, there's no in-between. If I am outside, it is against my will. But partly because I detest repetitive tasks. And mowing the lawn is the definition of a repetitive task. Up and down and up and down with the mower whirring away and doing that weird vibrating thing to my hand bones. No. Thanks.

My family has a running joke that if the laundry has made it from the hamper to the washer to the dryer and back into the closet in less than twenty-four hours, someone should probably call for help because Mom is clearly experiencing a medical emergency. It's not that I hate clean clothes or organized space but the thought of standing there for even ten minutes to match and ball socks, put blouses on hangers, or fold pajama pants enrages me. I hate laundry. Because it is repetitive. Same thing over and over and over and it never ends and about the time I'm finally done folding a load my family has had the audacity to wear more fucking clothes that I have to wash and fold and put away and fuck it we are all nudists now.

And then I repeat that same rant over and over in my head. It's a war I'll never win but also one I'll never be able to stop fighting. I have had the good fortune to reduce how often I'm required to report for duty at the front lines of laundry because I have children. My eldest daughter now handles her own laundry from start to finish. From the outside looking in that's because I mommed so good. I knew I was supposed to equip her with basic life skills—like knowing how to operate a washing machine and manage both her time and space to know when she needs to do laundry. It's a whole "prepared for the real world" teachable moment, right?

Wrong. I taught her how to do her laundry purely because I didn't want to do more laundry than I absolutely had to. If she is able to seize a life lesson out of my very selfish desire not to get into a fight with an impossible pair of artfully distressed jeans because I legitimately cannot tell if that leg is still inside out or not . . . so be it. Because I really hate doing laundry. Because I really hate repetitive tasks.

Which has certainly presented a challenge to my opting to parent my children responsively. As stated above, there is a lot of repeating yourself in parenting. Find me a parent of a child with verbal capability and a basic understanding of holidays who has not had the following conversation and I'll find you a magical unicorn who poops raspberry sherbet.

"Mom, is it [insert holiday]?"

"Almost. Just a few more days/weeks until [whatever the kid just said]."

"So it will be [holiday] soon?"

"Yep. It will be [holiday] soon."

"How soon?"

"Just a few more days."

"How many days till [holiday]?"

"Um, three?"

"How many days is that?"

"Yeah, it's just three. You can't count and I know that so that's why I said a few. Three is a few."

"So it's three days till [holiday]?"

"Yep. Still three days till [holiday]."

"And then we can have [insert vague description of holiday activity]."

"Yep. That's a part of [holiday]."

"But today is not [holiday]?"

"Nope, not yet."

"When can we [holiday]?"

And that right there is the point that even the most responsive, controlled, regulated parent threatens to cancel the whole damn holiday for the rest of ever. It feels like you're spinning in a circle of intentional ignorance. I'd wager that nine out of ten times this kind of circular discussion is not annoying because the kid is excited and trying to communicate that in the most pedantic way ever. It's annoying because we, as parents, are forced to repeat everything seventeen times.

Have you ever counted how many times you completed a specific action? I bet you have. We all do it. Especially if it's an action we don't particularly look forward to. I spent one day counting how many times my child asked me for a snack. My son asked me twenty-seven separate times. Keep in mind, I feed this child well. Three square meals, two balanced snacks, numerous bites and tastes of whatever I'm eating at any given moment, constant, unquestioned access to water, and standing permission to grab and consume any piece of fresh fruit in the house. My kids have an entire drawer in the refrigerator just full of their snacks. He's fine. He eats plenty. Didn't stop him from asking me for a snack twenty-seven times.

For my son and me, that repeating snack request was less about his nutritional needs and more about how a four-year-old tracks time. It took me months to figure that out. Typically shifts in activities happen in conjunction with a snack or mealtime. This wasn't necessarily by design, it's just how it sort of worked out. He knows that after the afternoon snack, I'm probably more willing to turn on a show or movie for him, or that the dreaded "rest or read" period happens after morning snack. So if he gets food, he can positively tell something in his routine is going to shift to something else. Essentially, I'm mostly sure he made his own snack-based clock.

But that's the kicker. While I'm over here being annoyed by the soundtrack of snack asks on a loop, he is gauging where he is in his own routine. And routine is just another word for complicated repetition. I can say I hate repetitive tasks till I'm blue in the face but I also thrive off routine. So do most kids.

Thus we return to the concept that parenting is a lot of repetition. Explaining things over and over again because they haven't grasped it or forgot is just a part of the whole ordeal. Kids thrive off routine so we repeat days on end. Get up, get dressed, get breakfast, get in the car, wade through drop-off line. The mornings look relatively similar. And when they don't—when a shoe has gone missing or a coat zipper finally gives up the ghost—that break in the routine, the repetition of the morning rhythm, has a rippling effect across the day. Routine is glorified, more complicated repetition. Remove the repetition and it just feels off.

Even our constant repeating ourselves does serve a purpose. Kid brains log information differently. They need the constant, repeated input. Sometimes it is because they "listen" differently than we expect. A child could be looking directly at you and be nowhere close to hearing what you just said. They were off in their own world, consumed by their own thoughts or what they were going to do before you tried to redirect their attention to you. Most often that difference in how a brain catalogues information is because adult brains are just better at braining. Plainly, they've had more practice.

Ever wonder why your kid can watch the same movie or series of television show endlessly? Admit it—one particular show or movie immediately popped into your brain and you involuntarily made a sound, face, or shiver of disgust. It's fine. That's normal. You endured what felt like eons of your kid entertaining a straight-up concerning obsession with one show or movie. Why are they like this? How is it possible that you were driven to the edge of sanity and they were still asking to watch it again? They are training their brains how to remember. The same thing goes with the book they always want to read, the song they won't stop requesting, or the activity that never, ever gets old. The constant repetition is part of the early meat computer programming, the early brain training.

As they get older they are less dependent on constant repetition. But that need for repetition, or reinforcement, never goes away. Not really.

Consider, for a moment, algebra. If you were educated in most parts of the Western world you probably took an algebra course or two in school. So solve this:

$$x/3 = (2x + 3)/7$$

I know damn well you straight-up told me "No" and came to this line to keep reading. Partially because this is not math time. Partially because the vast majority of us forgot how to do that. There was a time when that was important to know, but not many of us use algebra on a daily basis anymore. So that knowledge we once learned and retained slipped away. We lacked repetition of the concepts through use so we discarded the information. (The answer is x=9 by the way.)

And if you were in the vast minority of readers who gleefully went "Ooh! Algebra!" and solved it, what's it like to be God's favorite?

Simply put, algebra is the reason I'm going to be repeating concepts and ideas throughout the book. We need the repetition in much the same way our kids need the repetition. It helps us learn. It helps us remember.

TL;DR

Gwenna can't count, probably. Repetition is a part of parenting. For the good of both the parents and the children. Repetition is a part of parenting. For the good of both the parents and the children. This book will repeat itself from time to time because it's really important you remember some of the ideas. We remember through repetition. This book will repeat itself from time to time because it's really important you remember some of the ideas. We remember through repetition. Gwenna thinks she is really funny with this chapter summary.

· 5 ·

INSTAGRAM IS A FUCKING LIAR
AND PINTEREST CAN SIT ON
A PIN AND SPIN

The following chapter is going to feel really bold, as it was written by a woman who exists primarily on social media, but it needs to be said: Social media, in all its forms, is a powerful parenting resource, helps us build communities and networks with unprecedented efficiency, and is complete and utter bullshit.

All three of those things are true at once. We talked about how useful the internet can be when it comes to figuring out how not to eff up your kids in the previous chapter. That's still true. As true as it was a few pages ago. But also, it's not. It's not useful at all.

Confused? Same.

When my eldest was born, Myspace reigned supreme in the social media sphere. Facebook was barely keeping itself alive, Twitter was a literal infant, Reddit was on pretty much no one's radar, and Instagram was years from existing. If you wanted parenting discourse (or drama, as it were) online you'd have to turn to the Mommy Blogs. (When you read this, imagine this was said super dramatically with a lot of echo and boomy sounds.)

The Mommy Blogs were . . . something. A lot of them had really good ideas, some fascinating takes on real-time childhood development, and gave parents this fresh new feeling of not being so goddamned alone in the sea of kid shit they were drowning in. But many of them, for the sake of views, read times, sponsors, or entertainment value, accidentally reinforced a precedent of perfection. To be fair, they weren't the first to create this precedent. They just added to it.

Look back on the history of sitcom TV. *Leave It to Beaver* featured June Cleaver, the ever perfect cookies-and-milk mom. Every hair, ruffle, doily, and throw pillow was in place at all times, without fail. Lucy Ricardo of *I Love Lucy* and Laura Petrie of *The Dick Van Dyke Show* at least had some personality and got into antics, but they still always maintained the perfect home and never, ever lost their temper at their children. They might get a touch annoyed but they never lost their shit. Even when, as wives, they slipped a little, causing trouble for the sake of the plot, they always made it all better and wrapped every problem up in under a half hour. Name me any other show from the forties, fifties, or a good chunk of the sixties and it was more of the same. Moms of that era were all perfect. Fucking perfect.

Yes, that was just TV. It was only ever for entertainment purposes and how those shows presented women as wives and mothers had a lot to do with public demands and expectations. Times were different and so was TV. It was assumed, rightly or wrongly, that people were comforted with the presentation of perfect. I can't say if that is true or not but that's the premise the station executives and sponsors built content off of.

What I can say is that I believe it really messed with people's expectations of what it was to be a mom and maintain a household. Even as TV progressed and the plots and tropes more closely aligned with reality, there was still this set of perfectly solved problems. Then came the turn of the century, the rise of the internet, and the Mommy Blogs (more boomy sounds, thank you).

Mommy Bloggers turned Momstagrammers had unprecedented power to self-edit. Perfectly posed family photos in waving fields of heather or wheat or whatever the fuck the fluffy, wavy plants were gave the illusion that it was easy to be perfectly happy in every way. Mostly because those Momstagrammers didn't have to post the seventeen other shots of their children screaming, fighting, and stabbing each other with the wavy plant stems. They didn't have to own that they had to photoshop a non-screaming baby head from one shot onto the only other shot where the middle child wasn't doing something weird with his face.

They shoved the same mess we all live with just out of shot of their perfectly styled and aesthetic playrooms. They left out the stories of shoe-based meltdowns and feeling overwhelmed by their own progeny in many cases. (This is not a universal truth, of course. Please don't storm those same internet channels to tell me about this one internet mom who didn't do that. I know they existed but they were the extreme minority.)

Here's the thing: I don't fault them for that. Not directly. Again, the standing expectations surrounding parenthood left no room for imperfection or realism. If they openly admitted that they lost their shit and screamed at their kid, they'd be eaten alive. It was really a rock-meet-hard-place conundrum in the earliest days of social media. And while the trend of Insta-ready motherhood has definitely subsided in the last decade (hence *Momma Cusses* in all my filter-free glory) the stranglehold it has on social media is still pervasive.

Parents on social media want to share and see others' best moments shared. The highlight reels of parenthood. It's nice to know that someone has their shit together if not you. But being constantly shown only the good stuff messes with our brains. Whether we mean to or not, we, the consumers of the highlight reels, begin removing the reality that surrounds those Instagram pictures. We forget there are probably be-headed Barbies and a sink full of unwashed dishes just out of frame. We tend to view these social media moms and dads as the paragons of parenthood.

But there is no such thing as a perfect parent. No life is perfect, no matter how many putridly positive posts are made about it. One InstaMom's life as she presents it might be something you, personally, strive to attain. But it's not perfect. Not by a long shot. It can't be because we aren't perfect people.

Before I wrap this up with a neat little bow in under thirty minutes, it feels important to address the social media platform I find the most paradoxical: Pinterest. Pinterest has no right to be simultaneously as useful and as infuriating as it is. No website has ever personally victimized me as much as fucking Pinterest—and there are whole threads on Reddit dedicated to hating me as a person.

Let me describe for you my relationship with Pinterest. It was the summer before my daughter started seventh grade and we were looking for things to do that weren't more video games, sitting in the wading pool, or the Netflix catalogue. To Pinterest we turned.

There we found cactus cupcakes. Now, I'd recently started growing cacti at home and my eldest was amused by the concept of hugging a cactus. The mental imagery of a hug but with stabby-stabs amused her to no end. Thirteen-year-olds are really weird. These Pinterest-worthy cactus cupcakes seemed easy enough. The website even said you could use boxed cake mix and jarred frosting. So we did. Kinda.

We even went out and bought a whole cake-decorating set, the good, name-brand one. We baked our cupcakes (chocolate chip cake, naturally) and set about squeezing and piping and globbing on concerning amounts of frosting. When it was all said and done, the frosting tubs scraped clean and green frosting on everything, including things that were not cupcakes, we stood back to admire our work.

They looked exactly like not cactus cupcakes. The cupcake part was recognizable. Our frosting work looked like someone had put Oscar the Grouch through a wood chipper and he landed in the general vicinity of the cupcakes. The absolute definition of a Pinterest fail. We were both disappointed. The perception of perfection cut both my daughter and me off at the knees.

Now, logically, I knew there was no possible way for our cupcakes to look as good as the nifty, perfectly staged photo the creator added to Pinterest. The original creator likely had years of practice working with cake and frosting as a medium. My daughter and I had never so much as held a piping bag prior to attempting to make sugar goo succulents. Of course our skill levels would not match.

And yet I fell victim to the nagging disappointment that

social media would have you feel when things don't come out perfectly. Both the eldest and I looked at our hours of hard work and instead of enjoying the time we had spent together and the process of trying a new thing, we were disheartened by the results. Is that Pinterest's fault? Absolutely not. But this unattainable perfection accidentally reinforced by the nature of how and what Pinterest is definitely didn't help.

Ultimately, social media is an intrinsic part of our lives as parents. Whether we want to own that or not, it is an inevitable force on how, why, and in what style we parent. Even if you consciously choose to avoid social media, it's still shaping the culture of raising crotch goblins. The mechanics of why this is are multifaceted and best left for other experts to more adequately explain, but it is true.

So how do we combat this? It begins with acknowledging the falseness of social media representations. Even I am guilty of curating what I share online. It's not untrue, but it might not always be the whole truth. Part of this helps protect my littles' privacy, part of it helps truncate the mundane reality of day-to-day mothering into the most entertaining bits for public consumption. But not all of it is total, unfettered reality.

That's the most complicated way ever to say, "Take social media with a grain of salt."

Next we need to address our own internal mindsets. The illusion of perfection is just that, an illusion. A fellow parenting content creator, @dumbdadpod, once put out a skit that has stuck with me for years. In it he described this scenario where you are a perfect parent. You do everything right for and by your child. You never yell, you're always engaged, you set good boundaries and enforce them with both love and logic. You are their rock, their confidant, and their mentor.

One day you will still die. You'll leave them. And the only person who has always been what they need when they need it, meeting them where they were, will be gone. They'll have to live the rest of their lives without you.

Okay, that is very morbid and wildly fatalistic. Sorry to darken the tone there. But the point stands: No amount of perfection will ever be enough. That's the problem with perfection; it's a utopian idea. No matter how perfect something is, there's always one little thing that could be improved, one more boundary that could be pressed, one tiny little detail that could use a little more work. You could be a perfect parent but they'll still have to learn how to live in an imperfect world.

When we release ourselves from being Instagram ready at every moment, it's an instant relief of pressure. TMZ is unlikely to pop out of the bushes in a gotcha moment because your mom bun has fallen down the side of your skull and you still have yesterday's breakfast dried onto your sweats. We can give ourselves permission to take the easy road occasionally, to skip a teachable moment because we don't have the energy to fight that battle, to outright fuck up.

Messing up around and with our kids is, in and of itself, a teachable moment. A lecture-free one at that. When we make a mistake, we have the opportunity to apologize. We have the chance to show our kids how to own your mistakes, take accountability, apologize, and rectify what we can in the aftermath. That's not perfect-parent shit, that's good-human shit.

I have a reputation in our home as the "oven killer." I have accidentally murdered or irreparably damaged three separate ovens in one fashion or another. The first was by dropping a very heavy casserole dish on the door and bending the hinges beyond safe repair. The second was when I attempted to remove the electric coils to clean under them and wrenched half the mechanism out of place, rendering that burner eternally useless. And the third, the moment wherein my child dubbed me the oven killer, was the direct result of a less-than-stellar parenting moment.

My eldest was eleven and we had just moved into a new home. She was adjusting, we were adjusting. There were many adjustments happening. Being very eleven, she had developed this new and infuriating skill of requiring incredibly specific, step-by-step directions to complete any task she didn't want to do. If asked to load the dishwasher she would, in fact, put dishes in the racks. She would not, however, rinse them off first or empty the contents into the garbage or disposal because I said "load the dishwasher," not "rinse the dishes off and then put them in the dishwasher." Noodles dried onto a poorly rinsed bowl, old bits of salad, that baked-on tomato sauce on the top edge of the lasagna pan—not a drop of water was wasted on rinsing those. Straight into the dishwasher.

When I decided to confront her, I tried to go in calmly, coolly. Setting a boundary, explaining the issue, confirming that she understood what "load the dishwasher" entailed. But talking to preteens is really fun and easy. (It is not.) So when she hit me with "It's called a dishwasher. If it can't actually wash the dishes, why do we own it?" Well, that triggered me. Should it have? No. Probably not. Did it? Yeah.

I tried to pull my shit together, and despite knowing I'd not done that at all, I continued the conversation. I attempted to explain that dishwashers do wash, but they're not powerful enough to liquify leafy greens. Then she pulled out the "Well, that sounds like a you problem, really. Why did you pick such a wimpy dishwasher?" The edges of my vision started to blur a bit. Should I have dismissed myself, collected my thoughts, and calmed down? Yeah. Absolutely. Did I? No.

Instead I lost my shit and yelled at her. And I know this story started about ovens and shifted to dishwashers . . . stay with me, we're almost there. This particular discussion turned rage fest happened right after we walked in the door. I was still holding my bag and my lunch box was hanging from the crook of my arm. I, still gesticulating wildly, went to move the strap down my arm, catch it in my hand, and gently slide it across the kitchen floor; a move I'd done a thousand times before without a thought. This time with all the yelling and roaring and general parenting fails happening, I didn't close my hand in time but I'd already committed to the arm-swinging motion. This meant I didn't gently slide the hard-plastic-bottomed lunch box across the kitchen floor. I Nolan Ryan-ed it across the kitchen, pitching it straight into the glass oven door. It shattered, raining down little squares of tempered glass all over the kitchen floor.

The sound of shattering glass snapped me back to reality. Three years into intentional parenting and I was doing it again. I was making my problems her problems. Yes, we needed to discuss that attitude and work ethic, but not like this. I looked at my daughter. She was on the verge of tears. I looked back at the now sparkly kitchen floor and then back to her. Back and forth with increasing speed. Until she was tracking with me. Looking at the shattered glass and then meeting my gaze. I said the first thing that popped into my head. "Well, if the dishwasher sucks, I think the oven sucks more now." She laughed.

I then proceeded *not* to apologize. Why? Because I was still mad; at her for the dishes thing and her commentary about my dishwasher selection prowess. And at myself for losing it. I told her as much and said it would be best if we resumed the conversation once I'd had a chance to calm down. I channeled that angry energy into rage-brooming the oven door off the floor. Once that calmed me down I did apologize. I pointed out that losing my temper had come with a natural consequence. Not only had I made her feel bad, but I had murdered yet another oven. And we still had to find a way to have a reasonable, rational conversation about dishwashing noodles and why that's bad.

Could I have handled this dishwasher thing differently? Yes. In many, many ways. But it wasn't a loss. I got to show her how to apologize by apologizing. I got to let her watch me own my problem and deal with the consequences.

Had I been more present on social media at the time, that type of thing would never, ever have been spoken. But I can feel you nodding as you read this part. You've been there already. Maybe not at the cost of a third oven in your adult life, but you've lost your shit. You've yelled because you ignored that little voice in your head. You've let a feeling get control of your body and immediately regretted how you handled a situation. Social media doesn't let you see those very human, very vulnerable, very important moments of being both a parent and a person.

Instagram is a fucking liar. Maybe not a malicious one, but a liar nonetheless. Pinterest can really mess with our heads. Facebook is a cesspoolish hellscape of conflicting information and toxic positivity. TikTok, Snapchat, Reddit—name it and none of it's really real. It's real adjacent at best.

Don't let social media dictate who you are as a person. It can influence, it can educate, it can alleviate. It can't dictate.

Repeat after me:

I am not a perfect parent and that's okay.
I am doing my best and that's enough.
I am learning how to be a parent just like my kid is
     learning how to be a person.
Instagram is a fucking liar and Pinterest can sit on a pin
     and spin.

There. Feel better? Okay, onward.

TL;DR

Social media is the best. Social media sucks. Social media has given parents a wonderful way to connect, exchange ideas, and feel just a little less alone. It has also created wildly unrealistic expectations. Approach social media with caution and skepticism. Remember you are only seeing the very best, most curated moments of parenthood and it almost never represents the entirety of what parenting looks like. The icky, boring, messy parts are often cut out. Gwenna has destroyed a bunch of ovens.

· 6 ·

IT ALL BEGINS WITH YOU

You're still here. Excellent. Wonderful. Brace yourself. This next chapter is a bit of a doozy.

If this is not your first foray into the world of responsive, intentional, or gentle parenting, you've likely heard the following joke: "Okay, I'm out here responsively parenting, when do my kids start responsively childing?" Bad news, bestie. They don't. By the time they are good and responsive, emotionally well-rounded, and functionally stable, they aren't kids anymore. Sorry.

When I was first shifting to a more intentional version of parenting, the very first piece of advice I was given by a kind, if direct, soul was this: "You can't expect your kids to figure out how to climb down off their bullshit if you haven't climbed down off yours first." That might be a paraphrase but you get the idea. Responsive parenting your kids looks like responsive parenting yourself first.

If you're fresh to the parenting gig, you're in luck. Most

elements of responsive parenting don't really kick in until your child has a decent amount of speech. You can absolutely help your four-month-old identify what they are feeling, but that's less for them and more for you. It's like a practice round. It doesn't really matter in the grand scheme of things but that doesn't make it less important. That means from birth till talking (typically around two to four years old), everything you're doing is more about training your brain and recognizing your emotional process than it is priming their gray matter for anything.

Ope. Wait a second. I can feel you bubbling up with some protest. I know. Stick with me. I am in no way saying that you're off the hook with the emotional awareness jazz just because your little is *little* little. I am saying that most of the legwork you're doing on behalf of your precious little tater tot is shaping your brain more than it is theirs in the earliest days. It is really hard to discuss big feelings and deep breaths with a human still fascinated by ceiling fans. But as you practice emotional regulation and awareness, you are showing them how to do it. It won't stick. It won't feel like it's working when they throw those big tantrums mere minutes after you calmed yourself down in their presence.

Ever looked at your child who is actively screaming his little head off for no good reason and just sighed with resignation? How about putting that same child, still screaming as if he has been dismembered, into a safe-for-him space and walking away to calm down? Congratulations. You did the thing where you identified your own emotional state (likely frustrated, confused, and exhausted all rolled up into one) and took steps to regulate. It might not have been intentional, or maybe it was. But you did it. That counts. You responsively parented your very tiny person.

Responsive parenting is the long game.

Gwenna, great, but I think I'm too far gone. My kids aren't babies. I've got a middle school enrollment form lost somewhere on my dining room table—it's about them now, right?

Yes. And, also, no. Responsive parenting is about the parents first. I'm gonna break out an analogy that you're going to roll your eyes at. Do it if you must, but it is a great fucking analogy.

You know how, on an airplane, the attendants go through that safety brief before taking off? They tell you to please secure your mask before helping those around you. You can't get your kid's oxygen mask on if you're unconscious. Most folks trot this gem out in relation to self-care. But I'm not like other moms. Nope, I'm using it to call you on your bullshit.

If you aren't emotionally regulated, it feels kind of bold to expect that of your kid. (See previous chapter on perfection. You're not seeking perfection, just improvement.)

So we can agree that responsive parenting begins with you, the parent. I say we can agree because I'm not with you as you read this and can't hear your protests. Ha. Point to the author.

What does that look like in practice? It looks like giving yourself a crash course in all the things you hope your kid will be good at. Here's a baseline to work with.

Caution: The line of questioning you're about to read may feel overwhelming. Especially if you've never or rarely practiced this level of introspection before. What's more is you aren't necessarily going to be able to answer all these questions immediately. You might have to sit with some or all of them for some time.

It's okay to feel a little overwhelmed. It's okay to not know the answers. The more you consider these questions, the easier it will be to figure out those answers.

If, however, you feel wildly overwhelmed by looking inward for these answers or if the very idea of these questions triggers you, I would personally suggest reaching out for help outside yourself. Therapy and counseling can be extremely helpful, especially if you come from trauma or are among those working against your own upbringing and breaking those generational cycles of abusive tendencies or outright abuse.

Okay, everyone sufficiently trepidatious? Cool, let's look inside our feels, shall we?

I'm going to give you a scenario to play inside your head. Pretend you and your child are at a wedding. It's been a long day. You are tired and your child has crested straight past tired, through sleepy delirium, and is now resting comfortably in the land of "You will all regret this tomorrow." You look up and realize your child is standing at a table, eyeballing the beautiful wedding cake sitting there, adornments glistening in sugar and decadence. You can see those gears turning in her see-through skull. She is going to touch it. She is going to reach up with those sausage-roll fingers and swipe some frosting. You call out to her and tell her not to touch the cake. She turns, looks at you dead in the eye, and, without breaking eye contact, puts her whole damn hand on the side of the cake.

Okay, got it. Have you played that out in your head? Feeling some feels about this scenario? Here we go.

How do you decide what you are feeling?

In the cake situation, you probably felt frustration, anger, anxiety, resignation. Maybe some fear of being judged or having to explain why the hell your child's handprint is on the cake. But how did you know that's what you were feeling?

Can you feel small shifts in mood or emotion, or are you only aware of the big swings between extremes?

If it hadn't already been a long day before the cake incident, would you be less likely to feel the anger rising watching your child near the cake? Or would it have felt more like it just slammed into you the minute that grubby little palm hit frosting?

What are your biggest triggers? What are your smallest triggers?

Which bothered you more with the cake, the fact that she touched it or the fact that she definitely defied you to do it? Do you think you would have been as angry if she'd just touched the table and not the cake? Would you have felt differently if she hadn't looked right at you, indicating she heard you and still had no fucks to give about your thoughts on the hand/cake situation?

Can you feel yourself moving toward a bad mood, a blowup, or a meltdown? (We'll call this the red zone.)

If the cake thing were actually happening in real life, would this be the moment you lost it, scooped the child up, and carried her out like a football? The rest of the reception be damned, it's time to go home. Or would you opt to stay and just keep the child a little closer to you?

What things help you recenter when you feel yourself moving toward the red zone? What things make it worse?

Would it help at all if the bride were right there, watched the whole thing go down, and said it was no big deal and genuinely laughed it off? Would it make a difference if you knew the baker was right there and could immediately re-pair the handprint? Even knowing that those who would be directly impacted or most likely to be sad or mad about your child's cake-touching shenanigans were not upset, would you still feel pissed for the defiance alone?

If you find yourself in the red zone, do you feel completely out of control?

Let's say the frosting finger sent you over the edge. Is this a situation where once you start, you have to let it all out because you can't stop the flow of anger? Or do you have the ability to still recognize you're having a whole tantrum and can cool your jets a bit?

Do you feel drained, amped up, or something else after exiting that red zone?

Moving forward with your imaginary cake toucher, you lost your shit. Do you need to sit down or do you need to go for a run? Do you feel the need to ice your head in a dark room or throw hands with a pillow?

What emotional states do you find most difficult to be in? Which feelings are the hardest for you to work through?

Which feeling felt bigger watching your imaginary child destroy an imaginary wedding cake: anger, frustration, fear? Thinking about those three particular feelings now and reminding yourself there were no toddler fingers in wedding baked goods, which feels yuckier?

And, final questions to sit with:

When you are in an okay mood, what puts you in a good mood?
Would that also move you from a bad mood to an okay mood?

We'll wrap up this whole scenario with the bride thinking it was hilarious and even asking the photographer to get a shot of your kiddo touching the cake. No one is mad at you and you decide to stay because damn it, the kid got a lick, you want some cake too. You've earned at least that much. But you're still feeling that residual feeling and are struggling to get back into dance-party wedding-guest mode. What could you do to come back to the dance floor and move past the cake moment?

That was a lot. I get it.

You doing okay? Yeah, you are.

Once you begin integrating an awareness of how and why you're feeling what you feel, it gets easier to assess, decide if that's a good place to be given the situation, or adjust accordingly. Emotional awareness and its eventual by-product, emotional regulation, are skills that take practice. Again, it's okay if the idea of constantly having to question your feelings is overwhelming. I say totally subjectively and anecdotally, the more often I stop myself from going over the edge and losing my shit on my kid, the easier it gets. Like, 1 percent easier each time, but I'll take it.

Consider this. If you were to have to describe the color red to someone who has never seen the color red, it would be a struggle at first. Color exists only as a visual thing. It has no texture, sound, scent, or flavor. Sure, there are some flavors we associate with red, but those have nothing to do with their color. Make a cherry blue and we'd still recognize the flavor as cherry. (I know this to be fact because snow cones exist.) There would be some trial and error but work at it long enough and you'd find a way to describe that color.

When, a week later, you encounter someone who has never seen the color orange and asks you to describe it, it's going to come a little easier. Still some floundering to find just the right words but not as overwhelming a task.

Next week, here comes the guy who doesn't know yellow and it's going to feel more familiar and be a little more natural to describe yellow. By the time you get through the rainbow and are moving on to the variants like chartreuse and maroon, the challenge is still there but it isn't this really unusual experience of describing colors to people who don't understand what colors are. You're not starting from scratch, you're customizing the description to the situation.

Sorting out your own emotional range and by extension being ready to help your kids do the same is similar to these hypothetical people with the underexposure to color. The more often you find ways to name, understand, and work with your feelings, the better at it you get. Even though it feels wildly foreign the first time you have to come to grips with exactly what anger or joy or grief feels like.

I know this chapter is heady and you might be a little up in your feels. But you're doing good. We've got one more little bit to go.

So you've done the introspection thing. You're getting better, or at least more open, to how and why you're experiencing the emotions. You can identify the big feels and you're goddamn amazing at describing colors now. (Same—even writing that little section of the book I derailed myself for an embarrassing amount of time. I now feel wholly equipped to describe the colors to someone who has never seen colors.)

Now you gotta do the hard part.

Fuck, Gwenna, that wasn't the hard part?

No, that wasn't the hard part. Identifying and tracking your emotional state is a massive part of it. What happens next is regulation. And if you've never intentionally regulated your own fee-fees, it feels really hard. First, let's get some semantics out of the way.

Regulation is not the same as suppression. Please notice that throughout this chapter I have not said "get past, get over, or shut down an emotion." It's always working through or with. Cramming down a feeling to avoid working with it is not the same as emotionally regulating. That's called suppression and is generally frowned upon. It's okay to be mad. It's not okay to make that everyone else's problem. In the words of my good friend Tori Phantom, it's okay to be mad, it's not okay to be mean. Again, the more you practice, the more getting mad does not automatically put you in the red zone.

Once you've identified that you've got the big sad or mad or glad, now you get to find ways to bring all that over-the-top energy surging through your hormone-soaked brain back down to level, to the point where you are not wholly consumed with how it feels. We'll go way more in depth on this whole regulation thing in a couple of chapters but here's what you need to know right now:

The human brain is deeply unfair. We don't know as much about it as we know about all our other body parts. We are in control of it, kind of, but then there are other parts and processes that are fully outside our ability to control. Your breathing is more or less an automated process handled by your brain. You can go manual and control your breathing. You can even stop yourself from breathing by holding your breath. But that only goes so long. Either your brain will flip out, make everything hurt, and force you to take a breath again. Or you'll win, pass out, and your brain will go back to autopilot breathing.

Your emotions are similar. They are kind of automated in that we rarely consciously choose what to feel. We just sort of do. We can take control of it, however. And with time and practice, we can get really good at understanding and working with our feelings. Given enough of that time and practice, we can actually be super aware of our emotions. Think of free divers. They weren't born with the ability to hold their breath for twenty minutes. They trained both their lungs and their brains to be okay with that.

Your tools for training your brain are regulations. And they are hyper-specific for you as a person. In the back of this book is a whole appendix of co-regulations—regulations that you practice with your child. While those are geared toward helping your kiddo sort out their feels, they can be a good starting place in helping you find your own regulations.

Good news. You made it. You made it to the end of this chapter that almost made you feel bad.

Bad news. The next chapter is also hard.

Good news. The one after that, not so bad. Let's go.

TL;DR

If you're just starting out with responsive parenting, you have to first responsively parent yourself. Learning how to not just feel your feels but understand them, where they come from, and how to regulate them is the very first step in parenting your kids responsively. It doesn't matter if you are starting the moment your kid arrives on planet Earth, or if you have college applications somewhere on your dining room table. Get good at feeling your feels so you can be better equipped to help your kid feel and understand theirs.

7

YOU WILL STILL LOSE YOUR SHIT

To review, we're working on releasing ourselves from the expectation of perfection. We are beginning to identify our triggers, becoming aware of our emotional state, and learning how to calm ourselves down so we are better equipped to help our kids do the same thing.

Get ready for the truth hammer. This whole process is going to fail more than it is going to succeed at first. You are still going to lose your goddamn mind on the regular. Even when you're really, really good at it, like, writing a book about responsive parenting kind of good at it, you're going to lose your shit. On your kids. For the littlest, most inane reasons sometimes.

And that's okay. It really, really is. The perk of this is you get a fresh round of Mom Guilt to help you out next time.

Hold up, stop, Gwenna. Mom Guilt is a perk? I think the fuck not.

I get it. It feels weird to view Mom Guilt as a perk. Especially since the internet as a whole has absolutely demonized Mom Guilt. Don't get me wrong, she's awful. (I am here using my own reference to my Mom Guilt, who I named Alice. If you and/or your Mom Guilt don't use feminine pronouns, fair. But for simplicity's sake, I'm going to refer to her as Alice and use she/her pronouns.) But she is useful and yes, she is actually a perk.

When we discuss Mom Guilt, I strongly believe our language is imprecise. I actually view the mental gymnastics of feeling like I'm utterly failing at raising my children and will be the reason they need therapy as two distinct entities of emotional torture: Mom Guilt and Mom Shame.

Mom Guilt is that little bit of your brain that remembers every godforsaken mistake you've ever made or thought you made as a parent. She* catalogues all the mistakes, the failures, the lapses in judgment, and the "it was a good idea at the time" moments. And yes, on the surface, that seems awful. No one wants to retain that. We want to forget and move on.

I get that. But it's important to remember all those times we missed the mark so we can adjust our aim next time we are confronted with a similar situation. Mom Guilt hurts and can wield those remembered missteps as an absolute weapon, but she is useful.

Storytime: My youngest daughter was and is absolutely fearless. There is not an ounce of self-preservation in her little body. She could barely hold her head up and liked to be swung at a frightening pace. If she didn't feel like the baby swing was about to fling her into oblivion, it was not moving fast

---

* For the purposes of this chapter, I'm referring to Mom Guilt and Mom Shame as feminine because I, personally, personify them as my own gender. You can assign whatever pronouns to your Mom Guilt and Mom Shame as feel appropriate.

enough. When she got some locomotion skills down, she was the climber, the leaper, the jumper, the runner. My girl-child is the reason I had baby leashes. Traffic? Seems fun, let's play *Frogger* IRL! This trellis arch in the community garden? Spider-baby! Two inches of water in the bathtub? Concussions be damned, BELLY FLOP!

So when my littles were old enough to play on the playground, she was all over that. My little town has a toddler-appropriate playground. The equipment is a little lower to the ground, requires a little less grace and finesse to climb on, and the ground has that weird rubber/foam squish padding that somehow does not grow whole lab cultures of mold when exposed to water. My daughter beelined for the highest point of the playground and toddle-climbed right up. I'd been helping my son navigate a tunnel when I turned around to see my two-year-old straddling a support beam five feet off the ground.

Instinctually I screamed her name. It startled her, she flinched, and fell. Thankfully she caught herself before falling all the way to the ground and I was underneath her before her grip gave out. She was unhurt. I was more emotionally damaged than she was physically bothered by the whole ordeal. Not only had her ability to climb higher than I expected in the milliseconds my eyes were off her come as a surprise, but I was also acutely aware that had I not screamed her name, it was unlikely she would have fallen. I lost my shit and she almost bit the dirt as a result.

Man, does Alice LOOOOOOVE replaying that one in the last moments of consciousness before sleep. While it turned out okay, I could have been the reason for the broken arm or concussion or worse. All because I couldn't keep my shit together.

Right, Gwenna, that sounds awful. So how is Mom Guilt useful in any way?

Because Alice's constant reminders of that time I could have made a better choice help me remember to make a better choice. I am now far more aware of my tone and actions, especially when I discover my kids engaged in risky play. Jordan Peterson may have a tome of interesting opinions on things, but we agree in at least one arena; it's important to let our kids do dangerous things safely. My failure at that is catalogued by Alice and serves as a constant, if annoying, reminder to chill the fuck out before my anxiety causes my kids to leave that "safe" zone of doing dangerous things.

No, it isn't pleasant to live with endless reminders of all the times you messed up. But you can either let that drown you or you can learn to swim. You can use those messed-up memories as the catalyst to trying something new, reacting in a different way, choosing your words more carefully, or making a better decision for both you and your kids' well-being.

Mom Guilt is not the enemy. She is the meticulous, insistent overachiever who can make you a better parent. She's like a bitchy librarian. Her attitude kinda sucks but she never forgets anything and knows exactly where to find any resource in the library of your own parenting cock-ups.

Her cousin, however: she's the real demon to battle. Mom Shame is the bitch who makes us feel bad when or if we choose to wean our children from the breast. She's the same one who wants us to loathe ourselves for choosing formula if that's the choice we made. Mom Shame tries to wriggle into our emotional centers and make us miserable for choosing our own needs over our children's wants. She forces us to question the things we know, to second-guess decisions we confidently made, and attacks us for having basic needs, much less actually addressing them.

Mom Shame is the one who deserves the angst and ire, not Mom Guilt. Mom Shame targets us for no good reason. Mom Shame is everything that our insecurities, the perfection expectation, social media society, and the overwhelming responsibility of not raising an axe murderer would have us believe. She is the embodiment of all the things we feel the worst, most scared, most confused, or most anxious about.

So what do you do about all of that? How do you begin to accept that Mom Guilt can help? How do you get good at identifying Mom Shame? More than that, how do you tell Mom Shame to fuck right off? And while dealing with all this emotional turmoil and sorting, how do you ensure you're probably *not* the reason your kids will need therapy?

Apologies. No, I'm not saying sorry to you. I'm saying that saying sorry is step one in answering all those questions above. You will lose your shit. And that gives you a chance to say sorry. It might sound dramatic and just the tiniest bit cliché, but "I'm sorry" is one of the most powerful things you can say to your children. Remember the oven incident from a few chapters back? The apology was a critical part of fixing that. The situation, not the oven. That just took money and swallowing my pride long enough to explain to my husband how I broke the oven.

First, it shows them that you are not perfect, nor pretending to be. It demonstrates how to own your mistakes and acknowledge the damage dealt by losing your shit. When you apologize you are demonstrating that it's okay to make a mistake and how to apologize and recover afterward.

Second, it validates them as humans. Our kids are tiny people learning to person from scratch. When we lose our shit on them or around them, our feelings are valid, as are theirs. Apologies are a wonderful way to subtly say, "I see you and your feelings." It's okay to be in your feels sometimes. Even if that means making a mistake. It's not the end of the world to lose your temper. We're all human, we're all imperfect, and we will all lose our shit. That doesn't make you a bad person or a good person. Big feelings are morally neutral. What determines if we are a good person is how we handle ourselves and the situation after the shit losing.

That was a super long-winded explanation of apologies. Thanks for that, Gwenna. How do apologies appease the Mom Guilt and Mom Shame combo of doom?

Excellent question. Thank you for asking. Apologies soothe the sting of Mom Guilt because while she catalogues the blowup, she also catalogues the positive reinforcement of the apology. She associates the apology with the moment when your kid hugged you back after you had yourself a little fit. She ties the mistake together with the humanness of the moment.

As for Mom Shame, apologizing is something all humans have to (or at least should) do on the regular. It's harder, though not impossible, for Mom Shame to hold it over your head and trot that gem out to make you feel bad if you handled the blowup with grace and kindness, both for yourself and your kid. Doesn't mean she won't try. But it is much easier to tell Mom Shame to shut up and sit down knowing that your apology was a sign that you already acknowledged how you messed up. You don't need to relive the mistake because you took steps to clean up the aftermath.

FIELD GUIDE ENTRY: *The Failure Method*

I'm a big proponent of the failure method. While it isn't the only way to learn, it is a really effective way to learn. I learned to cook via the failure method. During my first marriage, I didn't know how to cook, despite my mom's best efforts to teach me in the years before I got hitched. We existed off a lot of microwave meals and those one-skillet dump meals from the freezer section. When I left my first husband and embarked upon single motherhood, that really wasn't an option, financially or nutritionally. I had to learn how to cook. I did this by watching an intense amount of Food Network and choking down a bunch of failed dinners. My finances were so precarious that if I burned the grilled cheese my options were to skip dinner or eat the burnt grilled cheese. There wasn't additional food in the house to simply make myself something else. It was a really good motivation to learn how to cook better.

Letting our kids fail is incredibly hard, especially when we can see that failure from a mile out. Sure, it's frustrating to watch my teen put off doing her English essay until the very last minute. I've been there. I've done that. She learned her procrastination from me. I'll own that. I know that both her paper and her stress level will suffer from putting it off so long. But it's important that after a few gentle reminders to get cracking on that writing, to let her dig her own hole. It feels almost cruel to step back and watch your kid fuck up. If our job as parents is to parent ourselves out of a job, part of that is letting our kid feel failure when we are still there to help pick up the pieces.

We have to let them fail safely from time to time. It normalizes that it's okay to mess up, figure out where things went sideways, clean it all up, and try again, hopefully in a different way this time. And learning how to fail when they are young and still have the direct support network of their parents and family makes it less daunting to fail when they've flown the nest and are out there fighting the patriarchy unattended.

This isn't to say that we always let them fail. Sometimes it's okay to intervene before things go off the rails. If limb, life, or major property is at risk for their failure, feel free to step in. I'd encourage it, actually. If you're at a point where you can't be there to help them process something that didn't go as expected, it might be wise to course correct with them. Honestly, if you're on the edge of your own emotional wherewithal and just don't have it in you to cope with the tears and the disappointment, go ahead and help out. But if the actual damage is going to hit their ego, feelings, grades, or plans more than anything else, let it ride.

TL;DR

You will definitely lose your shit with your kids. Your temper will get the best of you, you will not be able to regulate, and you'll blow up and make mistakes while raising your kids. That's okay. Each mistake you make in parenting is an opportunity to learn for next time and to apologize. Apologies are vital to raising good humans. Mom Shame and Mom Guilt are not the same thing. Mom Shame makes us feel bad for doing things we need to do for ourselves, like taking a break or addressing our basic needs. Mom Guilt catalogues and reminds us of our mistakes so we can adjust and avoid making the same mistake over and over again. Mom Guilt hurts but with purpose. Mom Shame just sucks.

8

MOMMA NEEDS A TIME-OUT

Okay, Gwenna. To be honest, I feel a little bit like shit. I have to be emotionally regulated, accept that I won't always be emotionally regulated, know that I will still lose my shit. And I have to become friends with my fucking Mom Guilt. I'm about thirty seconds away from throwing you across the room.

Yep. I get that. Your feelings (which I totally made up and decided are yours based solely on how I felt when I was first working through my own shit) are valid. But you're okay. This is the last chapter that is going to focus on you. And it won't feel like twisting the knife. Because this chapter is going to send you to time-out. But that's a good thing.

My childhood home was a monument of the late seventies' and early eighties' appreciation for the color brown. I mentioned this before but feel the need to really drive home the brownness of my childhood home. When my parents purchased their unfairly affordable two-bedroom home with a den where the garage should have been, my dad felt the urge to build himself a shrine to brown.

He put in brown carpet in the living room, a muddy chocolate shade. The bedrooms rocked a deep tawny carpet with specks of sepia that made them look perpetually dirty. In the kitchen, a lovely patterned Berber carpet with mandalas of absolutely no meaning danced across the floor adding pops of chocolate, mustard yellow, and a muted, dull burnt orange to the beige palette. Yes, carpet in the kitchen. It was lovely. Half the cabinets were tan plywood with a butcher block top. The other half were a throwback to the kitchen of the future, oatmeal-colored rolled steel topped with laminate counter with sparkly lines running through it. Sparkly taupe lines. I didn't even know taupe glitter was a thing. It is. Apparently.

The living room, dining room, and den were coated with faux wood paneling. It absolutely screamed "trailer park but fancy." Which made sense, as my dad had spent a not insignificant part of his childhood raised in a trailer. I guess it made it feel like home to him. And only him. The kitchen walls were pink because that's what my mom wanted. And they painted their bedroom a weirdly depressing peach. How peach ends up depressing, I don't know, but they found it. Maybe it wasn't the peach paint. Maybe it was the dark, heavy wood-framed waterbed that made it depressing. Maybe it was that my parents' relationship was deeply and intrinsically flawed. No way to tell, really.

The furniture, curtains, throw pillows, and blankets. All. Fucking. Brown. My childhood was really mud colored. Weirdly it is not my least favorite color despite the near war-crime levels of its application in that house. My least favorite color is a silvery gray. Why? Because my whole childhood home was a shade of sepia—except the spot by the front door. We weren't bougie enough to have an actual entryway or foyer. The front door of the house opened right up into the cocoa-themed living room and my mom peeled up a rectangle section of the carpet and put down a silvery-gray peel-and-stick tile. It made it feel a little more *entrez s'il vous plaît,* I guess. Those peel-and-stick tiles were also my time-out spot.

I hated time-out. Those entry tiles my mom selected had the slightest bit of texture on them. A bit like unsanded, un-weathered stone slabs. Tiny shelves of elevation that I still re-member the feel of some thirty-ish years later. I'd have taken a spanking over a time-out any day.

Again, I was raised in the eighties and nineties, wherein parenting styles weren't quite as defined or discussed. I got my share of whoopings and spent a good bit of time in time-out. Knelt down on those silvery-gray peel-and-stick tiles, my nose pressed into the corner, the front door on my right shoulder, the brown paneling on my left. The brown door trim ran down the side of my face, always leaving the faintest little indent as I pressed my face into it. That part wasn't required. I just liked the sensation of the rounded wood corner on my cheek.

Time-out didn't do shit for me. I was simply counting sec-onds that lasted hours until the timer went off. One minute for every year of life. That was my sentence. Here's the thing though: If my kid brain couldn't convince me not to do a thing because I lacked impulse control or it hadn't occurred to me that it was wrong to do in the first place because I was still learning to person, a time-out to "think about what I'd done" wasn't going to make any of that make sense.

The time-out as a disciplinary method is kind of iffy as far as the science goes. According to Dr. Daniel Siegel, a clinical professor of psychiatry at the UCLA School of Medicine and co-author of *The Whole-Brain Child* and *No Drama Discipline*, time-outs are a form of social exclusion. Using brain-imaging research, he noted that social exclusion and the sensation of physical pain light your brain up in similar fashions.*

On the other hand, separating your kid from the trigger, the overstimulating space, or the sibling that is trying to un-alive them by attrition has its perks. We'll discuss more about time-outs and other consequences in a later chapter but for now, let's leave it there. Time-outs can be a good separation.

When in time-out, I either knew I'd broken a rule but couldn't help myself or I was unclear on the rule in the first place. Kids don't often need time-outs. Not the way I received them. You know who needs time-outs? Parents. Remember, responsive parenting starts with you. You have to be in control of your emotional state if you want your children to learn to be in control of theirs. Of course, we are human and that's not always possible. Because damn kids have a way of homing in on exactly what can drive us over the edge. They don't just push our buttons, they know exactly how to find them and go full HULK SMASH on the whole fucking emotional-trigger control panel.

I propose a new application for time-outs. Well, not new, I suppose. We'll say different from the time-outs of my child-hood. If your kids are losing their shit and it is pushing you to lose yours, place your possessed child in a safe place, give them something to distract them, and put yourself in time-out.

Give yourself permission to admit that you are overwhelmed

---

* Daniel J. Siegal and Tina Pane Bryson, "'Time-Outs' Are Hurting Your Child," *Time*, September 23, 2014, https://time.com/3404701/discipline-time-out-is-not-good/

and underregulated. Give yourself space to step away and assess how and why you're feeling overwhelmed and underregulated. It's acceptable, and I'd argue occasionally necessary, to put yourself in time-out.

A parent time-out will naturally look different than the time-outs I (and probably you) received as a kid. A little less kneeling, potentially more counting. It is your opportunity to remind yourself that

1. They are kids. It is their job to push boundaries.
2. They suck at peopling and it's a part of your job to help them learn how to people better.
3. Your boundaries are still valid even if they push them.
4. It is okay that this made you feel some type of way. Your feelings are not invalid simply because you spawned a brood.
5. If you want them to stop pushing this boundary, you have to explain that.
6. If you want to explain that without losing your shit, you have to find your level space.
7. Fucking breathe.

Use the chance to take some deep breaths, get a drink of water (or whiskey, I won't judge), maybe eat a piece of fruit while you process your own emotions. This is that "starting with you" routine. Use whatever method works best for you. Deep breathing, a few stretches, screaming into a pillow, fidgets . . . whatever allows you to feel your feelings in a safe, nonconfrontational way is the correct way to level yourself out and make the most of your self-imposed time-out.

I routinely joke that I bully myself out of bullying my kids.

Laugh or scoff if you need to but if it feels like nonsense but it works, is it still nonsense? Remember that Mom Guilt who reminds us of our mistakes? During my Momma Time-Outs, I have whole conversations with Alice, my Mom Guilt. I let her remind me of past mistakes and take the opportunity to improve on those missteps. They look like this:

"Last time I didn't cool my jets before addressing the problem, I made the girl-child cry and the boy-child made me cry. There were many tears because I couldn't keep my shit together. So this time, aim for one less crying human in the mix and we're making progress. Don't be a douche canoe and make the same mistake twice. You are better than that. You are not a douche canoe. Now grab your breakdown by the vulva, take a deep breath, release the rage, and go parent good."

It's like a really weird locker-room pep talk. Except instead of sitting in a locker room full of my teammates, I'm probably leaned over the kitchen sink rage-chewing carrot sticks and mumbling to myself.

Some children will give you the span of thirty whole seconds to work through this process. Others will allow a more generous two minutes. But you are allowed to communicate your own boundaries and needs with your kids.

"I know you need help/feel bad/want attention, but Mommy/Daddy/Parental Unit needs a minute and I need you to respect my space."

The bonus of this whole adult time-out business is that by communicating to your kids that you have a need for space, time, or both, not only are you taking care of your emotional well-being but you are demonstrating how to communicate that need. Will your kids respect that request? Maybe. Hopefully. And the more often you do it, the better about it your kids will get. But they won't always. And that's kind of a sucky truth of parenting. Parents have real needs and kids won't always give a damn.

Remember your kids learn so much more from your actions and behavior than they do your words. In the writing world we call this "show, don't tell." I could tell you how a character was feeling.

"Bella felt anxious."

Or I could show you.

"Bella swallowed hard against the lump in her throat, her fingers twirling a strand of hair with a desperate ferocity."

I still described anxiety but this time you probably felt a little of that anxiety yourself. Same principle in parenting.

By demonstrating how to communicate your needs and then following through with the necessary steps to meet those needs, you are priming your littles' gray matter to be able to do the same as they become more emotionally cognizant. Even if you never sit your children down and explain what you're doing and the lesson you're trying to teach them, consistently and constantly demonstrating it accomplishes the same thing.

FIELD GUIDE ENTRY: *Time-Outs for Kids*

Occasionally, I do put my kids in time-out. This happens most often when the standard methods of calming down or co-regulations (these are discussed more in the next chapter) aren't working and my kid is pitching an outer-space-sized fit. I'll invite them to hang out in a specific spot and take a time-out.

This looks a little different from the time-outs I got as a small-ish human. First, there is no kneeling, nose pressing, or timers. I don't drop them in time-out and leave. I actually sit with or near them while they have space to scream, flail, or proclaim that I am no longer their best friend. There is no set time limit on this "time-out" beyond when they are calm-ish. If it takes them two seconds to stop banshee screaming, then that's all the time-out they needed. If they choose to hang out for twenty minutes, so be it. They needed that time to themselves. (That has literally never happened, but the option is there.)

Sometimes a book will be offered, or a drink of water to nurse. Occasionally, if it's pretty close to snack time, I'll bring them something to munch. Fidget toys are popular as well. And lovies (all my children have one) are a must. This also isn't my go-to. It's a last resort most of the time.

I'm not asking them to think about what they've done or demanding they self-regulate. I'm simply giving them a space to feel their feels without any expectation of anything else. Typically I end up opting for this when everything else has failed and they just need to be really, really mad. The feelings are never the problem.

FIELD GUIDE ENTRY:
Parental Time-Out Vs. Self-Care

The term "self-care" is cursed. So cursed there's a whole chapter in this book dedicated to debunking the myths surrounding what it looks like to take care of yourself. But here we need to be sure we are communicating clearly. A parental time-out is not necessarily self-care. It might borrow some principles from it. You might use similar techniques like yoga, breathing, or snacks as both your parental time-out and as self-care, but they are not interchangeable. Here's a handy chart comparing the fundamental differences because I like charts and it feels like adding charts to a book on parenting is something a writer of books on parenting would do. Even if that writer is very much not a parenting expert because who is the best expert on parenting your child? Yes. You. I told you I'm going to keep reminding you of that.

TL;DR

Time-outs can be useful even in responsive parenting. But they are less for the kids and more for the parents. Giving yourself both permission and space to step away means you have a better opportunity to regulate your feelings and get yourself just a little calmer before trying to address the child and whatever problem they created that got you all up in your feels in the first place. Gwenna's childhood home was really brown. She emphatically describes how much she was not a fan of this.

Parental Time-Out	Self-Care
Often unplanned timing	Intentional timing
Emotionally focused	Emotionally and physically focused
Seeking to restore level thinking	Seeking to relax and recharge
Lasts only as long as needed	Lasts a planned/predictable amount of time
Works best without kids present	Can happen with or without kids present

9

THE BIG FEELS LOOP-DE-LOO

S trap in, bestie. This one is a long one. And for good reason. If you only read one chapter of this whole book, let it be this one.

Kids' brains must be an absolute disaster to be in. When I watch my kids play, it seems like they have two states of operation: all the stimulation, information, and thoughts all at once, DO ALL THE THINGS!; and "the rest of the world does not exist." Thinking about what it must feel like to sort out their own thought processes exhausts me.

It's also wildly unfair that children have as much energy as they do. The time in a human life span one has the highest energy is also the time of one's most limited understanding of what to do with all that energy. Children manage to be the most resilient and fragile creatures simultaneously. They fall over, eat pavement, stand up, and keep on playing like nothing happened. Ten seconds later, a doll's shoe stubbornly won't go back on properly and an entire screaming breakdown ensues.

Why? Because feelings are hard.

In responsive parenting, that "feelings are hard" bit is important. We can help our tiny humans with those feelings by laying down a bit of groundwork. Kids thrive off routine and predictability. Even in those times wherein they are nothing but spontaneous and wildly unpredictable, if you watch closely, you can see their own micro routines forming. They play the same game and prefer to have defined rules, even if they are making those rules up.

Even how to handle big feelings can be a bit of a routine. Here's the cycle I've employed often to guide my children through a big feeling. I call it the Big Feels Loop-De-Loo. The "big feels" part is pretty self-explanatory (although, to be fair I'm going to spend the whole chapter explaining that), but the "loop-de-loo" part of the name, that one's less obvious, I think.

I've found in myself, in my kids, in my kids' friends, and from anecdotes shared with me by total strangers and clinical

Big Feels Loop-De-Loo

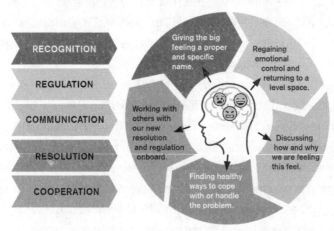

RECOGNITION

REGULATION

COMMUNICATION

RESOLUTION

COOPERATION

Giving the big feeling a proper and specific name.

Regaining emotional control and returning to a level space.

Working with others with our new resolution and regulation onboard.

Discussing how and why we are feeling this feel.

Finding healthy ways to cope with or handle the problem.

professional alike, the process of feeling your feelings is not always linear. You might hop from step to step, skip a few, go backward, go to the next one and loop around like the world's shittiest, most emotionally charged carnival ride. That's okay. That's normal, especially as you are first using this process to sort out the big feels as they come. Eventually you (and by extension your kids) get better at it. At some point, it becomes almost a subconscious or second-nature process. Think of it like emotional muscle memory. The more often you do it, the better you get at it, and the less conscious effort is needed to work through the Big Feels Loop-De-Loo.

RECOGNITION

In order to know how to handle the emotion, you have to be able to identify both the feeling and the cause. For adults this can sometimes be challenging because humans often feel more than one feeling at once. If you're cooking something and accidentally touch a hot pan, you'll probably feel pain, fear, frustration, anger. You might also get a few waves of shame, panic, confusion, delirium, or mirth. That's a lot of feels all at once. Being adults with fully developed brain bits (namely, the amygdala and hypothalamus) means we can cycle through all those things fairly effectively, if maybe not quickly.

The same happens for kids, but they lack both the immediate awareness and vocabulary to name how they are feeling or sometimes what triggered that feeling. That means when they encounter a problem of some sort, we need to help them practice identifying and prioritizing what they are feeling. You can't respond to a feeling if you can't even identify what it is.

At the earliest ages (between twelve and twenty-four months, give or take), the best a responsive parent can do is try to accurately name that big feeling or the source of the tantrum. A screaming child is having a feel even if it's over a really minor reason. (Note: It's minor to us with our big adult brain. It's not minor to them. It's very, very major to them. That's part of that whole immature brain thing.) You can offer up a name for that feeling and normalize it. That's the very earliest part of recognition. "Oh, did you throw your toy out the car window? And you're mad that the toy is gone? Yeah, I'd be mad too, buddy."

My daughter has firsthand experience with the loss of a toy to childhood impulse nonsense. There was a time that she lived and breathed *My Little Pony: Friendship Is Magic*. She knew all the things about the ponies, the lore, the drama, the world. It was, for a time, her entire identity. The gods help you if you called a "pegasus" a "unicorn." There's a difference. And heaven forbid you mislabel an "allicorn." What's an allicorn? A pony with both a horn (a unicorn) and wings (a pegasus).

Her favorite pony was a pegasus (it had wings) and she carried this doll with her everywhere we went. The blue-and-rainbow pony figurine was her emotional support pony, I swear. One day, her brain went, "Stick her out the window so she can fly." So she did. My daughter, with seven years' life experience, stuck the action figure out the car window, while on the interstate, traveling a mere seventy-five miles per hour. The wind ripped that little pegasus right out of my daughter's hand. I didn't even see it hit the ground it was gone so fast. Thankfully it didn't hit another car.

There was no turning around. There was no trying to fetch it. It was just . . . gone. And my daughter's world momentarily collapsed. To me it was just a goofy blue horse with wings. To my child, it was a precious possession. I immediately thought to myself, if it was so important, why did you yeet it out the car window on the damn interstate? But the risk of losing it never entered her mind. She wanted her pegasus to fly. And fly it did. Away from her. And out of her life. Forever. She was crushed. And no amount of "it's okay to be sad" was going to make it better. Her doll, her winged horse with the rainbow glitter tail was gone. I had to let her be sad for a time. I still had to help her name the feeling and let herself feel it, sit with it, endure it, and move on from it.

We did eventually make it to the store and she got the upgraded version of the pony. And we had the chance to discuss why we keep our shit *inside* the moving vehicle. So, bonus physics lesson in the mix.

As they get older and learn to speak, you can get more specific with the words.

"You seem really frustrated that you have to brush your teeth. Frustration is fine. Tooth decay is not."

I've never been one to shy away from big words. It feels doubly important to provide our kids the language to communicate their feelings. See the feelings wheel below for good ways to introduce more specific terms for emotions.

On the other side of the coin you might be able to identify the emotion, but not the cause.

"You seem like you're really sad. What gave you the big sad, sweetie?"

"That is a whole lot of nervous coming out of one little dude. What's got you scared?"

Personally this is my least favorite scenario; when I can tell they are emotional but have no idea why. I find these the hardest to recognize because triggers come from everywhere. It could be the monster in their closet. It could be they remembered their superhero shoes from three years ago and are suddenly overcome by grief that they don't have those superhero shoes anymore. Sourcing the feeling can be the trickiest.

For kids, everything feels of relatively equal value. They love the expensive toys just as much as the cheap dime toys they get in their Happy Meal. Value is assigned almost entirely by emotional response, not dollar value. While adults do that for some things, especially heirlooms or keepsakes, we also tend to be more careful with the stuff that costs more or is harder to get. This makes figuring out why a kid is in the throes of grief or rage or jealousy or humiliation next to impossible. Sometimes we have to stop at just figuring out the name of the feeling, move on to the next step, and hope the source makes itself known at a later point in the cycle.

And we have to accept that feelings can be hard, unpredictable, and sometimes flat-out inexplicable. Ever woken up in a bad mood for no good goddamn reason? Everybody does. Everybody, including kids.

Eventually naming the feeling for them will shift to "Can you tell me how you're feeling?" Or "How does that make you feel?" Reminding them to recognize and identify their emotions will become standards of communication over time. The more often you encourage them to name their feelings, the more you show them that this is just part of having them.

Ultimately, as with all things in parenting, there will come a point where you won't need to help them recognize what they are feeling in that way. They'll be able to recognize they're feel-

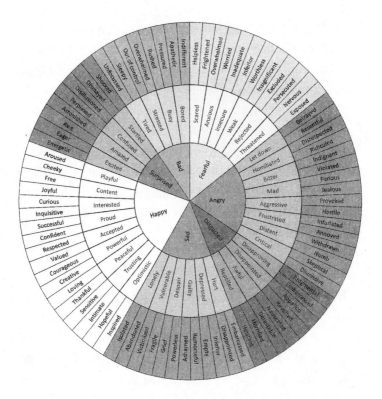

ing some type of way, put a name to it, and decide what pushed them to that point.

REGULATION

After you've recognized what and hopefully why your kiddo is in a big feel, now you need to help them return to regular. This doesn't mean stop feeling the feel.

There have been several studies that point to cortisol, the stress hormone, affecting both the ability to pay attention and the ability to remember information.* Stress is confusing, as sometimes being under stress *improves* our ability to remember stuff. But in the case of heightened emotions, big feelings, or flat-out tantrums, we don't remember stuff very well.

One of the phrases that helped me immensely as I relearned how to deal with my children's tantrums was "Tantrums don't need to be stopped. They need to be worked through."

Say you walk into a store to pick up a box of diapers. When you get to the register, the cashier informs you that the credit card machine is down and they are taking cash only for the moment. You don't happen to have cash on you. Your options are to return home empty-handed or go to another store. There's no way around it. You're going to be mad. Now, because you're a grown-up, you aren't going to take it out on the cashier. But you're probably going to throw yourself a nice little tantrum in the car. Your steering wheel is going to hear all about it on the way to the next goddamn store. There might be some light flailing and bouncing in the car seat. The seat belt might get just slightly abused. Does that make you immature?

No. Not at all. Tantrums, to some extent, are a part of regulation. Uncomfortable feelings beg to be released. That often starts as a tantrum, no matter what age you are. Questions of immaturity only begin to wander in if you can't stop the tantrum or you make that tantrum someone else's problem. Adults probably have the emotional control to let themselves have a tantrum, release some of that energy, and then move into solving the problem or addressing the source of that

---

* Susanne Vogel and Lars Schwabe. "Learning and Memory Under Stress: Implications for the Classroom." *Science of Learning* 1, 16011 (2016): https://doi.org/10.1038/npjscilearn.2016.11.

tantrum. That's called self-regulation. If they lack that, that's called being a Karen.

Kids may be able to do that some of the time. We, as their parents, simply need to give them space to attempt to feel a feel and regulate themselves. A child struggling to operate a spoon who gets mad, screams at the soup for not staying on the spoon, and then tries again has technically self-regulated.

Other times kids get so far into their feels they lose the ability to reason their way through an emotion, or the emotion is new or bigger than they've regulated and they struggle to maintain their emotional control. After the eighth time of trying and failing to get the soup to their face hole, that same kid who self-regulated moments ago loses it completely, chucks the bowl to the floor, and collapses into complete emotional dysregulation. Aka a full-blown meltdown.

Their brains get soaked in both adrenaline and cortisol and no valid thought is being processed. Logic is out the window and it's all hands on the tantrum deck. In my girl-child's specific case, emotional dysregulation comes in the form of not only screaming and whinging but arguing for the sake of arguing. Potential solutions are as dissatisfactory as the initial problem.

She gets upset that her ponytail is messed up and collapses into a full-blown tantrum over it. If I offer to fix her ponytail, she gets madder. What about just taking it down? Nope. Made it worse. Leave it be? Absolutely not. She is over the edge and the world is ending.

This is where co-regulation comes in. When your kid gets to the place where they've lost all control, you can step in and help them center themselves once more. This looks like a lot of different things. There's redirection, distraction, safe place, isolation, deep breathing, and a hundred thousand other methods. Which ones will your child respond to? There is absolutely no way to tell until you try. Different types of emotional outbursts or tantrums might require different types of regulation. The more often you co-regulate with your tiny human, the quicker you'll be at recognizing what technique is going to help the most.

For ease of reference, I've created an appendix of co-regulation ideas at the end of this book. Take a look. Try a few. Modify them to your needs and your kids' preferences. If a co-regulation got everyone back down to the space where communication was possible, then it was a successful regulation.

Final note on regulation: Co-regulation is for both of you. Remember in the previous chapter when we discussed getting triggered by your own children? Tantrums are definitely a lot of parents' triggers. Especially if their own mood or emotional state is nebulously controlled at best. If you find that your kid's meltdown is on the verge of sending you into one of your own, it's time to co-regulate. Even if your kid wants nothing to do with you woo-sah-ing in child's pose on the kitchen floor, they are still watching you handle your shit in a healthy way. Many times just demonstrating a non-screaming way to calm down is enough to quell at least the worst of the pterodactyling.

COMMUNICATION

Once everyone is back to a regulated place, now you can start working through the problem. Remember the problem is not the feeling.

The communication part of the Big Feels Loop-De-Loo is where you have the opportunity to figure out why there's a big feeling if that wasn't readily apparent. It's also the point wherein it's most important to remind your child that feelings are good, even the uncomfortable ones. Big feelings are never by themselves problematic. They are normal, acceptable, expected, and in many cases a good thing. Being angry isn't bad. Anger can absolutely be used as a motivation to solve a problem. Fear is an indicator of an unmet need or dangerous situation.

This is also when we address where handling that feeling went awry. It's the postmortem of the temper tantrum. Until you get through the regulation step (or more likely coregulation), the communication part is bunk. Dr. Kristyn Sommer, a researcher on children's early cognitive, social, and emotional development and fellow parenting content creator out of Australia, explained the anatomy of a tantrum as an arc.

There's the trigger: the thing that sparks a big feel. Next comes the buildup. This may be where your kiddo attempts to

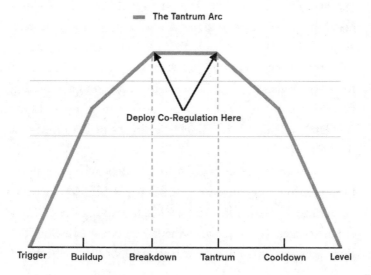

The Tantrum Arc

Deploy Co-Regulation Here

Trigger   Buildup   Breakdown   Tantrum   Cooldown   Level

self-regulate and it's your first opportunity to try to head off the tantrum before it goes nuclear. There's a brief window for communication here.

If that doesn't work and they still get all worked up, either with the biggest of big feelings or a new feeling they've never processed before, you end up in breakdown and tantrum zone. At that point you're into the regulation section from above. Communication becomes ineffective at best, impossible at worst until you get back to level. Even in that cool-down stage, trying to talk about the "hows" and the "whys" of the feeling might get you and/or your kid worked back up.

Once you've got everyone regulated (yourself included), it's time for the talky bit. Communication is where all those life lessons and emotional growth happen. You can address any problematic or ineffective ways your little chose to handle a situation or a feeling and offer better solutions.

Communication is less about solving the problem and more about accepting and processing the feelings the problem exposed. I've said this before and I'll say it again: The feelings aren't the problem. It's okay that a small thing caused a big feel, although how they expressed that big feel might have technically been an overreaction. Now that we've felt that big feel or found out what triggered it, we can work through accepting that feeling, decide if that was the appropriate response to the problem, and determine if the big feeling helped us or made it harder to solve said problem.

Exactly what you communicate will depend on the situation, the child, the intensity of the tantrum, and whether this is a feeling they've defined and worked through before or if this is a new one. (In other words: They've been mad before but this particular flavor of mad is frustrated, or they've been sad before but this time it's more a feeling of loss they've never had to explore before.)

But here's some baseline discussion points for communicating about feelings. Tailor these questions to fit your actual communication style and the general comprehension level of your toddler-shaped rage vessel.

> What are some things we can do when we start feeling [insert name of emotion you identified in recognition]?
>
> How did you react to this feeling? Do you think that helped?
>
> What are some other things we can do when we feel [emotion]?
>
> Do you think doing [X/Y/Z] could have helped before we had a meltdown?
>
> Was there a point you could tell you were losing control that you could have asked for help in this situation?

Word of caution on the communication front: This part of the Big Feels Loop-De-Loo has a limited window. There may come a point at which communication stops being heard and it turns into a lecture. Once that line is crossed, your kid is likely tuning you out. Personally I struggle with not getting lecture-y. I'm a talker and I like words. Sometimes I say too many.

RESOLUTION

So we've gotten all the way here. We've named, felt, regulated, communicated; all that's left is deciding what happens next.

Resolution could involve brainstorming solutions to the problem at hand together or separately. It could be trying again immediately, this time armed with some new solutions or ways to try. It might look like walking away, giving some time and separation from the problem before giving it another go. It very well could mean giving up entirely. That's not necessarily a bad thing.

Maybe your kiddo isn't ready to eat soup with a spoon because it's hard and their fine motor skills aren't quite there yet. Potential solutions could look like trying again, this time with a little less frustration getting us all shaky and sloshing the soup out of the spoon. It might be getting a straw, using some bread or crackers to thicken it up and make it easier to spoon, or just pouring out the broth and eating only the chunky bits. Maybe it looks like pouring it out (or back into the pot depending on your level of tolerance for both food waste and sharing food previously touched by another human) and enjoying pepperoni and cheese sticks for dinner. That's for you and your small human to decide. Whatever your solution is, talk through it and decide what feels right for the situation.

COOPERATION

This last bit of the Big Feels Loop-De-Loo is one that won't be a part of the ride every time. Cooperation is only needed when someone else was involved in the meltdown. Perhaps the trigger was a fight with a sibling or classmate. Maybe there was a blowup at your spouse, partner, or co-parent over the soup issue. When another party was involved either directly or tangentially, cooperation is the last part of the resolution.

It is important that you establish a resolution before you begin chatting about cooperation. Equipping your kid with the logical processing to decide how to handle a problem as well as processing their emotions is the missing critical element in this whole process. The younger they are, the more focus has to be on their emotional processing and the solutions that will help them not only with the problem at hand, but equip them better for the next time they encounter a similar issue.

But once those things are established and conversations had, you can address how to handle the other parties when they are involved. That might mean discussing an apology. In our house a lot of times it looks like recommending everyone find a new game to play because this one is causing undue stress. Maybe it's redefining the task at hand so that everyone's roles are better defined and understood. Again, a lot of this feels so vague in written form because each problem and associated meltdown are going to require different approaches.

Remember, much of parenting is throwing spaghetti at a wall and seeing what sticks. The beauty of understanding the Big Feels Loop-De-Loo means you don't have to throw the whole pot. We're back to those "responsive parent" artisanal noodles.

FIELD GUIDE ENTRY: *Forced Apologies*

When my husband and I first started toying with the magic three-word phrase in the earlier parts of our relationship, it wasn't hard to admit to each other that we were in love. We began expressing our feelings toward each other in the same way everyone else does.

"I love you."

"I love you, too."

It took about three times of that for me to be dissatisfied with the response. "I love you" is a fine thing to say, but "I love you, too"—that bit felt wrong. It felt too automatic. Too blasé. It wasn't the right way to respond to the love of my life reminding me that he loved me back.

And there it was. "Love you back." This was and is our special way of acknowledging that the other's profession of adoration is both heard and requited. It didn't feel forced or as if it was said in passing. It was intentional.

And the intention, the purposefulness of "love you back," is the most important part. We aren't saying it because we feel obligated to reply to "I love you." We're saying it because we mean it.

The same goes with apologies. The words "I'm sorry" are just words, and words only have the power we give them. When "I'm sorry" is said automatically or because someone told you you're supposed to apologize, the words lose their meaning both in the saying and the hearing.

But how do you teach kids to apologize without telling them, "Go say sorry!"? First, we demonstrate it. We apologize to our kids when we mess up. We apologize with an audience if necessary. We apologize to our partners. We apologize to inanimate objects (that might just be me). Kids learn far more from our actions than our words.

Second, we incorporate the idea of an apology into cooperation. In our family that looks like this.

"You were mad and you hit your sister. That hurt her. If someone hurt you, how would you feel? What should you do when you hurt someone? Yep, you should say sorry. Would you like to apologize to her for hurting her?"

Nine out of ten times the kid will wobble an oversized head at me, wander over, say sorry, and offer a hug. That tenth time when the answer is an emphatic "no," I'll remind them that everyone feels better when they apologize, the person who was hurt and the person who did the hurting. I won't force them to apologize but I give them all the reasons and opportunity to do so.

FIELD GUIDE ENTRY:
Preverbal and Early Verbal Big Feels Loop-De-Loo

For kids who are attempting their earliest words but not quite able to fully communicate, responsive parenting feels the most like wheel spinning. They don't have the words to tell you exactly what's wrong, just that something is. And they lack both the attention span and the comprehension skills to work through most healthy coping skills. So how the hell do you be a responsive parent to a child in that middle spot of "aware but not with the program"? Everything discussed in the previous chapter is valid but maybe not fully applicable.

Your cycle looks a little different. It's rather simplified.

Recognition, Regulation, Reinforcement, Redirection, Repeat

Recognition: You can name the big feeling for them.

Regulation: Help them calm down if needed.

Reinforcement: Redefine the boundary they crossed and that it was unacceptable to make those choices.

Redirection: Offer them something to detach or distract them from the stressor.

Repeat: Keep doing this over and over and over again until you're pretty sure nothing is working and you're utterly failing as a parent.

Take biting, for example. Your kid gets frustrated and bites you. Name the feeling ("I know you're frustrated . . ."); remind them of the boundary (". . . but teeth are not for biting. Teeth are for smiling. They are for eating food. They are not for eating people."); bring their attention to something else ("Can you hold this spoon for momma? Show me how you use the spoon!").

And then keep doing that same endless cycle what feels like seven hundred times a day. If you feel like you are about to explode both literally and figuratively, congratulations, you have a preverbal toddler. Keep doing this until they just grow out of the damn biting stage. The more words they develop, the less the biting feels like a valid form of communication. The older they get, the easier it is to communicate with them and the more you can foster that emotional development. It's just a matter of time.

And remember, as with all the worst stages of parenting, this too shall pass. They won't be this age forever. And it is 100 percent not required to love every moment. You're allowed to hate some of them too. Especially the teethy ones? Seriously, no one has ever fondly recalled being bitten by their child. And if they say they loved it, they are masochistic or lying. Or both.

TL;DR

I'm not going to give this one to you. No, I'm serious. I know chapter summaries are supposed to sort of wrap up the chapter and give you good chewy nuggets to digest. But, this is probably the most important chapter of the book. Go read the whole thing. No skimpy-skimming this one. The Big Feels Loop-De-Loo might be a silly name but I think it's really important. So important, it is the topic of the biggest chapter in the book by far. No TL;DR for you. You're gonna have to go read this one. And then maybe read it again. Sorry, not sorry.

10

BOUNDARIES ARE MEANT FOR BREAKING

When my eldest was younger, she was a tiny little explorer but only of things just out of her reach. She cared for absolutely nothing at ground level. That is to say that if I deemed it safe enough for her to play or engage with, she wanted nothing to do with it. The myriad of toys bought specifically for her enjoyment and enrichment? Nope. All the goos, salves, creams, and oils in Momma's makeup collection seem way more fun. The play kitchen I bought and proudly presented to her one Christmas? Fuck that thing in particular. There's a whole REAL kitchen for the using. Mountain of kid-centric, harder-to-destroy books? Oh no, there's a vintage copy of *The Hitchhiker's Guide to the Galaxy* up on that very top shelf that definitely needs attention.

She was also pretty fearless when she decided she really wanted something. Ask her to climb something high at the McDonald's PlayPlace, absolutely not. Voluntarily scale the refrigerator while

Mom tries to cook dinner? That's where it's at. Once she learned to walk, all bets were off. I babyproofed everything. She took that as a personal challenge. I had to get really good at creatively babyproofing. I couldn't use the plastic-and-silicone latch things from the big box stores. She could defeat those like some safe-cracking, super-spy baby. I had to invent a complicated cabinet-locking mechanism using a scarf, a zip tie, a dowel rod, and some duct tape. I could open it. She couldn't. I won. I kept a large cinder block in the bathroom for nearly two years to keep her from playing in the "duck pool." That's what she called the toilet after accidentally knocking a rubber ducky into the bowl once.

(Disclaimer: Please do not use a cinderblock to keep your toilet seat down. That honestly was a terrible choice and could have resulted in greater injury to my child than her just playing in the toilet water. Luckily, it didn't, but all the same. Cinderblocks are not babyproofing tools, generally speaking.)

And then it started happening—the shift. I accidentally walked away from a cabinet without resecuring the scarf/stick mechanism. When I returned, it was untampered with. She no longer cared. She defeated my closet-door locking rig one morning and instead of flinging all her clothes across the room, she simply picked out a single outfit for the day. Potty training began and the cinderblock moved back outside. One cobbled-together rig by one, the babyproofing was no longer necessary.

What most of us call babyproofing is a very early version of setting boundaries. Yes, some babyproofing is to protect the baby from itself (like corner guards or pool noodles around the fireplace hearth), but most of it is to prevent babies from getting into spaces or items not safe for them. It is the first version of boundaries our children experience, most of them in physical form. Not only are they probably told, "Don't touch the bottles under the sink," we physically prevent them from opening the cabinet door with locks, magnets, alarms, or scarf/stick thingies.

The eldest was about seven when I stood staring at my entertainment center. It was just a crappy flat-pack stand with a shelf and enough room for an okay-size TV. It had moved with us at least three times, a post-divorce purchase of necessity that never got upgraded with the rest of the furniture. And it still had a single clear plastic corner guard attached. It had been years since it had actually been needed. By that point all the rest of the babyproofing had faded away, the contraptions long disassembled or abandoned to the whims of the apartment complex we'd moved out of. But this one corner guard remained, the last bastion of when boundaries were physical, visible, and coated in safety foam. As I peeled it off the cheap plywood, a chunk of matte black veneer came with it. The last of the babyproofing was gone. The boundaries and safety guards were totally on me.

Honestly, boundary setting for your kids is pretty easy when it comes down to it. You use your adult brain to decide your kid is not big enough, dexterous enough, or careful enough to do a thing, handle an item, or be in a place. So you say, "No. Don't do this." And you keep saying that over and over and over because while boundaries are really easy to set, kids more or less don't give a fuck.

As kids get older, boundaries are more than just a set of dos and don'ts. Boundaries are the first taste of a kid being able to determine their own needs as well as the needs of others. Essentially, it is their first lesson in empathy.

Wait, Gwenna, you want me to believe that my desire to not let my kid drink the Fabuloso purple drink under the sink is going to teach empathy?

I mean . . . kinda . . . yeah. The first boundaries we set with all the babyproofing and denying our children the apparent instinct to off themselves in innovative ways is mostly about preserving them and keeping them safe. As they get older, the boundaries begin to protect other people (or their things) as well. A seven-year-old is unlikely to try to eat the makeup palette but they will absolutely destroy it while playing with it. So setting the boundary "Don't touch Mommy's makeup" is more about preserving Mommy's things, not protecting the kid from the makeup.

It's a valid boundary and at first glance, it is simply protecting Mommy's makeup. But it is also an opportunity to discuss the "why" of boundaries. Why do we want to protect something that isn't ours? Basic human decency, to start with. But as luck would have it, we are born without the knowledge of how to be "decent." That's a learned skill. It also involves deeper sociological issues like community versus self-preservation, societal and cultural norms, the shifting mores of the technological age . . . it's complicated. And low-key kind of boring.

I'll poorly wrap it up like this. Humans, out of necessity, are born pretty dang selfish and needy. Babies cry to alert us to a need, most of the time a super basic one like hunger, the need for rest, or cleanliness. But they also do not have one flying fuck to give about the needs of others. They don't care that adults cannot adequately function off three nonconsecutive hours of sleep. They couldn't give a rat's ass if their provider has eaten or showered or pooped. When they have a need, it's always urgent and must be addressed immediately. Instinctually they scream until this need is met or attention is provided.

As they get older it becomes their caregiver's job to teach them how to be less of an asshole about their needs while also showing them how to meet those needs on their own. As the crotch fruit gain speech, dexterity, the knowledge of how to hold and control their bowels and bladder, some needs stop requiring a caregiver's assistance. But we still have to teach them how to be aware of the space, the humans around them, and the situation. We teach them to respect the belongings and bodies of others. Even at a very young age, we accidentally teach empathy.

"Teeth are not for biting people" was a very common phrase for several years in my home. My youngest spawn are only two minutes apart in age and both were speech delayed. (Thanks, weird twin things + global pandemic.) That meant that once the pterodactyl screeching was not being heeded, in their heads the next best way to tell their sibling to piss off involved early-stage cannibalism. "Teeth are not for biting people" is a boundary based entirely on empathy, because it is a boundary set for the well-being of another human. The boundary isn't "Don't be mad" or "Don't express your anger." The boundary is "Don't hurt someone else because you have a big feel."

We present it this way: It's not okay to take your emotions out on someone or something else. It is especially not okay to hurt them, damage them, or draw blood in the expression of that big feeling. Kids aren't born knowing this. We teach them. With boundaries. That demonstrate and encourage empathy.

My children being twins did not uniquely equip them to bite each other. A lot of kids spend some time in the biting phase.

And if it's not biting, it might be hitting, kicking, scratching, pinching, rage-puking, or holding their breath. These are very common and developmentally appropriate behaviors for toddlers (for the purposes of this we'll define "toddler" as somewhere between twelve months and three years, give or take a few months). We'll chat more about developmentally appropriate behaviors and how to handle them responsively in a later chapter.

Once you're past the babyproofing boundaries and the first flush of empathetic boundaries, you enter the stage of conditional boundaries. "Don't cross the street until you look both ways." "You can't move on to another toy until you put the first one away." "Empty the dishwasher before you go outside." "You can say 'damn' in the house but you should never, ever use it around Nana." This version of boundary setting is less firm. It isn't a strict "Do this, not that" boundary. It's a "Use your situational awareness and decide what to do next" boundary.

Now here's where you get a confession. Until I started parenting responsively, I never viewed those "use your judgment" parenting moments as boundaries. But that's what they are. We set a parameter of behavior and help our kids abide by that boundary. In my head setting a boundary made me Gandalf standing on a strangely skinny rock bridge screaming "YOU SHALL NOT PASS" to my fiery hellbeast children. And in some cases that's true. I vividly remember my mother walking out of the sliding glass door of my middle school bestie's home yelling, "Gwenna! Get down off that roof right now!" The boundary that I not climb on and then jump off roofs was one I fully understood and chose to cross. My mom had her Gandalf moment there. But most of the boundaries we set as parents fall into the conditional boundary territory.

While you didn't ask for my opinion on this matter, you're reading my book so ya kinda did. In my opinion these are the best boundaries because they force the kid to employ a few critical thinking skills while processing what happens next. It primes their little developing brains to begin probing for what-ifs, assess risk, and play out scenarios in their heads. Remember as humans we are born considering only our own needs and, later, wants. We have to learn how to be patient, communicate, and eventually meet our own needs, and meet those needs in such a way that respects that other humans also need to live not only on this planet but in proximity to us.

As adults a good chunk of our boundaries are conditional. Yes, we still have some empathetic boundaries. It is frowned upon to maim another human being no matter how big a fartknocker they are being. Speed limits allow us to remain situationally aware while ensuring the safety of others around us. Casual Fridays are a conditional boundary for many folks in professional environments. We rock the power suits and pencil skirts Monday through Thursday and break out the sexy jeans and comfy top on Fridays.

To recap, not only do boundaries protect our kids (often from themselves), our property, and the health and well-being of those around us, they are also lessons in empathy and situational awareness. We spend the first twelve or so years defining almost every single boundary for our children or allowing teachers, coaches, mentors, or other professional child wranglers to set those boundaries for our offspring. After that, we've hopefully equipped them with that empathy and situational awareness to begin experimenting in setting their own boundaries.

So, all that said, how do you decide what boundaries to set, and if and when to move them, and how do you communicate with your crotch fruit that the boundaries are important, not arbitrary, and for their general health and wellness?

Excellent questions. And disappointment incoming. There's no one way to do any of those things. There are hundreds of thousands of ways to decide what boundaries are important and millions of ways to get your child to understand the importance of those boundaries.

The easiest boundaries are those that ensure safety, like those babyproof sticky tabs and cabinet closures. They are boundaries that center on protecting that tiny chaos goblin from cutting their own life short. After preventing accidental death and/or dismemberment, it gets muddier.

Deciding on boundaries comes down to some important and individual concerns.

Are there legal implications for enforcing the boundary? In the US, education is compulsory and while there are options for educating your child ranging from public schooling to unschooling, you still have to take certain steps to provide for and prove your child is learning how to read, write, and 'rithmetic.

Are there religious or philosophical reasons for the boundary? For instance, kosher and halal dietary rules are guided by religious and philosophical principles.

Are there family or societal values that are important to learn via boundaries? In our family we allow cursing when we are confident that our children understand the meaning and impact of the words they choose. But for some families, there are long lists of words that are absolutely taboo and should not be used under any circumstance.

Are there cultural taboos/mores or regionally acceptable

practices you wish to enforce or resist? Whoopings, chanclas, groundings, using the "guest" towels, sitting on the plastic-wrapped couch, strict bedtimes, dark sodas, what to do when there's more milk than you want to drink but not enough for a full serving for the next person . . . these are often dictated by personal experience of your region, culture, and upbringing.

Is there a family history that makes this boundary important or a history of generational trauma this boundary helps prevent? "Never go to bed angry" is an important family value that makes perfect sense to us but may not be feasible or necessary for all families. And that's okay. It means that we will sacrifice a bit of sleep to work through an emotional problem and it's okay that other folks need that night of sleep and rest to properly work through to resolution.

The best I can offer is this: I hate traditions. "Tradition" is a word that, in my semi-Southern upbringing, means "We've always done it this way." When it comes time to celebrate or practice a certain tradition, I wrinkle up my little nose and ask, "Why? Why do we have to drink a quarter gallon each of eggnog on Christmas Eve?" If (and inevitably when) the answer ever comes back "Because we always do," it has stopped being a tradition and has become a habit. If however, the answer still has meaning and impact on our lives, well, pour me some eggnog, I guess. This same line of reasoning applies to boundaries and helps us decide when and if to move them.

Now because I know you're curious about my wildly specific example of Christmas Eve eggnog when discussing traditions, STORYTIME! It's one of my favorites. Once my parents divorced, we often struggled financially when I was growing up. Eggnog was a luxury not often afforded on our shoestring budget. But Christmas Eve was special. Christmas Eve we got eggnog from a local dairy called Braum's, and spun it up with a mile-high pile of whipped cream from the can and a generous dusting of nutmeg. Even on years that I knew full well Santa couldn't come and there'd be no gifts under the tree the next morning, my mom found a way to get us our Christmas Eve eggnog. I haven't lived with my mom in over two decades but every Christmas Eve I pour myself a glass of eggnog and, when possible, call my mom. I still have a "why" and probably always will.

If you can still identify that your little one needs help remembering to make safe choices, respect the space and possessions of others, or use their situational awareness to decide the best course of action, that boundary is still important. But when the point comes that they can successfully make those decisions, consciously, it might be time to move the boundary or lift it entirely. I don't remember at what point I could stay out roaming the neighborhood with my friends past dusk, but at some point the boundary of "Be home when the streetlights come on" was lifted. (Yes, I was a child of the eighties and nineties. Cell phones weren't a thing. No, I don't know how so many of us made it to adulthood.)

The explanation doesn't have to be complicated or multifaceted. The decision to hold and continue to enforce a boundary could be as simple as "I'm not ready to let them do that." Or "I can't rely on my womb fruit to make the right decisions consistently." That's enough. As long as you've really considered why the boundary exists, checked your own bias on their growth and maturity, and periodically check that the reasoning still stands, you're good, even if your peers have lifted the boundary in their homes and lives.

Ultimately our goal in setting, enforcing, reassessing, and

resetting boundaries is this: We want to equip our children to be able to do the same for themselves. Remember we are attempting to parent ourselves out of a job. This means that as often as possible and as they are able to comprehend, you explain your reasoning for the boundaries you set. When they are little-little (preverbal and early verbal), the "why" is still important but less likely to be heard or understood. But as they get older, it's really useful for kids to get the reasoning behind the boundary. Remember they have limited autonomy. Much of their first twelve years of life they get told where to be, how to dress, what and when to eat, and what they are do-ing with their time. We sort of trickle that autonomy out. So anytime you find yourself needing a boundary, when you can explain why you can't let them use the roof as a diving board, it helps them learn risk assessment and mitigation.

Of course that takes time and repetition, but they do get there. Eventually. And hopefully with a minimum of broken bones.

FIELD GUIDE ENTRY: *Repeat Rule Breakers*

Strong-willed. Driven. Trying. Unruly. If any of these words trig-gered you it's likely because you've described your own child us-ing one of these terms. You have a child who seems intrinsically attracted to finding and breaking rules. It doesn't seem to matter what options you give them, how many times you explain yourself, how much effort you put into making sure you have their atten-tion and that you're using language they understand. If there's a boundary, your little chaos goblin will cross it.

Chances are pretty great your child needs one of two things.

1. They need you to reassess and redefine the boundary. If your toddler routinely scales the baby gate and gets into the kitchen, no matter how many times you reinforce the gate or tell them that's an unsafe choice, it's probably time to remove that boundary and find new and innovative ways to protect your child from themselves. Yes, that's more work, but your child is communicating that this boundary has reached its efficacy breakpoint. That doesn't mean they are ready for full, unfettered access to the butcher knives. It just means that the boundary needs to scoot just a little further out. If you've got a teenager who can't seem to get themselves in the house by curfew, you might want to adjust that curfew. But Gwenna, they are already having an issue abiding by the rules we set, why would it make sense to give them *more* of what they want? Yeah, it feels absolutely nonsensical to give more when they are already "taking" more than what we offered in the first place. But I want you to stop and ask yourself, why is this particular time important? Will they turn back into a pumpkin after 10 p.m.? Or is that just the line you drew because it felt right at the time? Why aren't they making it home on time? Probably poor time management, if we're being honest. But rather than drill down and shame them for those time-management skills, give them a range and a reason to be home at a certain time. You can incentivize that time-management skill development. Rather than a hard boundary of "Be home by 10 p.m. or else," give them a window and ease the stress just a wee bit. "Be home between 10 p.m. and 10:30 p.m. If you make it in the door before 10 p.m., I'll do this thing or contribute to this thing, or let you do whatever is on your list of stuff you really want to do or accomplish." Whatever will motivate them

to watch the time and plan for travel and incidentals just a little better.

2. They need something to do that allows them to contribute in a meaningful way. I'm loath to compare childrearing with having a dog, but damn it all if this analogy doesn't work perfectly. If you have an active, intelligent dog breed and don't give them an outlet for all that energy, they will find something to do. You may or may not like their activity of choice. It could be destroying pillows or digging up the whole of your backyard, but they will find ways to release all that pent-up hyperness. But when you start taking them outside and letting them run themselves ragged chasing a ball, or start training them for agility or tasks or tricks, those destructive, hyper behaviors will begin to wane and eventually fade away. I hate that I'm going to say this in all earnestness but your kids will do the same. If your child is constantly and consistently finding ways to push and cross every single boundary, find another way to give them reason to abide by the boundaries. Find a task or job that ties back to the boundary that's just so tempting to cross. Can't stop pulling out every dish from every cabinet they can reach? It's time to introduce the "help Mommy unload the dishwasher" game. You unload the breakables and sharps and let them have at the rest of it. It doesn't matter if they get them back perfectly at first. But by allowing them to help you're valuing their contribution to the family/household. More important, you're demystifying what lives in both the cabinets and the dishwasher. There is less reason to explore if they are already fully aware of what is behind those cabinet doors or inside the magic water-whirring box.

TL;DR

Contrary to popular opinion, responsive parenting consists of creating and enforcing just a ton of boundaries. But no boundary is permanent. What begins as elaborate methods of literally locking things down with babyproofing tools turns into your kids just understanding a no-touching zone. Boundaries are also one of the first ways we teach empathy. Deciding to respect a boundary is deciding to respect the person who set it and we learn that as children. That means as parents we have to teach that. Also, Gwenna tried to make you cry with a story about eggnog. She hopes it worked.

· 11 ·

NO

Alrighty. You are nearing the halfway point of the book and you're still here. Mental health check. You doing okay? Feeling some feels? Asking some good questions? Good. Good. I've got great news. This chapter is going to be a very relieving and freeing chapter. Because we're going to talk about doing one of the things many parents are naturally very good at: saying "no."

Kids are born with a strong self-preservation instinct. Hence all the crying, warbling, howling, and screeching in the newborn stage. They act as though if they don't absolutely lose their shit, food will never be provided, attention will be intentionally withheld, and their needs will never again be met. The child could be watching you prepare their bottle or have their bums being actively wiped and they are still screaming like you're never going to be able to resolve this problem for them.

Then they gain some sense of mobility and all of a sudden that self-preservation instinct seems to bury itself in some deep, inaccessible part of their brain. Once they are ambulatory all bets are off. They go from caterwauling resource gobblers to mildly suicidal ninjas with awful risk assessment skills and a preternatural attraction to things that will definitely maim or kill them. As a result parents quickly pick up the skill of saying "no" a lot. Like, a lot a lot.

And, as with all things having to do with raising children, the minute we get really good at predicting when they are gonna go for the forbidden Kool-Aid (Seriously, what child-free genius thought an attractive shade of purple was the best choice for a particular low-cost cleaner?), the child evolves. And we have to balance this need for keeping them from offing themselves to letting them experience the world in their own way. That "no" we got so good at yelling across the house at a child who has just discovered how tasty a power cable looks dwindles in use.

Then we enter the first flush of "responsive parenting" and things get even more confusing. Validating their emotions while regulating yours, allowing them to explore their own boundaries, experience natural consequences, metering the actionable consequences (more on that later . . .) and suddenly "no" feels like a taboo word for some.

If I've said it once I've said it a thousand times before and will say it a thousand more, responsive parenting is not permissive parenting. Even as a responsive parent you can and absolutely should tell your child "no." Just straight-up, nope, bad idea, kid, back you and your tongue away from the wall outlet.

You probably just finished that whole chapter on boundaries. And a lot of the times the boundaries we set are dependent on "no."

"No, you can't pet the wild bobcat. Kitty not friendly. Kitty has murder mittens."

"No, you can't eat only marshmallows. Not how biology works. You need protein and maybe something green."

"No, you may not play *Frogger* in real life. Respawn is not available on this level and I promise those eighteen-wheelers hit different."

But I want you to reread those ridiculous examples. Notice anything important about those "no, you may nots"? It's cool if you didn't notice. Every single one provides a "why," a reason why this "no" is important. That's the difference between responsive parenting and other child-rearing styles to me—the parent's explanation of the "why" and the child's buy-in.

We want our offspring to develop those situational awareness skills, the risk assessment, and to rediscover the self-preservation instinct they put on pause in the earliest toddler days. In order to do that most effectively, we, as parents, are beholden to explaining ourselves, especially when preventing our children from doing something that seems really fun at the moment. Essentially we try to avoid the "because I said so" explanation.

My mom was a "because I said so" mom. Not every time she made a decision would she trot out the "because I said so." And not out of malice or a lack of care and compassion. Occasionally she would explain why she made the decision but I, being stubborn and indignant, would press her for more in the hopes I could sway her "no." "Because I said so" was a surefire way to get me to wrap up the whinging. But she was also a product of her own upbringing. She didn't exactly subscribe to the "children should be seen and not heard" mentality (much to her own mother, my grandmother's, chagrin) but she did believe that children did not necessarily possess the capacity to understand the workings of an adult brain. And to some extent, that's not wrong. Kid brains are not as developed. No, they aren't going to be able to realize, rationalize, or conceptualize the same way as an adult.

But on the other hand, that ability to reason through, assess risk, decide on the best course of action isn't a setting that activates at some magical point of development. It is a learned skill that takes time and practice to master. There are adults with fully developed brains who struggle with this. So when we take the time to explain why we've made a decision on our womb fruit's behalf, we are giving them the tools they'll later use when it's their time to think through a decision.

As a child I absolutely despised "because I said so." First, it always followed a "no, you may not" so my hackles were already raised by not getting what I wanted. Second, not having any other reason than my mom's apparent whims was irritating. I know now she always had a reason and might have been able to explain that, but perhaps not in a way I'd have grasped. And again, her own childhood affected her perception of motherhood. I vowed rather young never to use "because I said so" on my children. I can brag that even prior to shifting to a more intentional style of responsive parenting, I cannot recall a single moment where I did not formulate a reason I had to decline a request or prevent an activity. Not that it hasn't been wildly tempting given that my children are my children and just as argumentative and insistent as I was at their ages. Nevertheless, I've resisted the insta-shutdown of "because I said so." Point, Gwenna.

That does lead us to a rougher part of responsive "nos." Explaining yourself can be tricky. And the younger your little is, the more you have to break down all that adult reasoning. You know you don't want to lecture them or make them feel silly for asking or trying. But you also don't want to info dump and talk over their head. Or frighten them. Or create a new anxiety. Which is a thing I accidentally did with an over-explanation.

My eldest was about seven and I'd only recently started with the whole responsive parenting. We'd just moved to a new house and she finally had a bedroom door. (Our previous apartment strangely didn't have a door to her bedroom. We'd moved in without one and ended up moving out two years later without a door. I never knew why.) One of the first nights, we put her to bed and as we were walking out, we closed the door behind us. She did not like this one bit. It wasn't a matter of being afraid of the dark, as we'd later figure out. It was that she found our chatting comforting and the soundtrack of fall-ing asleep.

Wanting to give her all the information, I outright told her, "We close doors because if there is a house fire, that door might buy you just a few more moments to climb out of the window. It's just a safety issue." She replied with a simple "Oh." It would be months until we figured out this little bit of infor-mation had accidentally triggered in her a near-irrational fear of house fires. Whoops.

So there is a line that we have to figure out. Unfortunately it isn't just one line, it's thousands. How much does your kid understand? How much do they need and how much is too much? And you'll have to make that assessment at every turn. Move a boundary? How much of your reasoning do you ex-plain? Decide not to let them go to that one kid's birthday party? How do you explain this in a way they'll follow? I can't tell you that. Sorry. Once again, you are the best parenting expert on your child(ren). And, as evidenced, you won't always get it right. And that is more okay than it feels. I promise. Oversharing, overcommunicating, under-communicating, confusing them . . . all possible. Being a kid is harder than we remember. Being a parent is harder than we expected.

These explanations don't have to be lengthy and detailed. Sometimes "No, don't touch the hot stove, you'll burn yourself" will suffice. And not all ages or individuals are going to follow the whole "No, you can't go over to your friend's house because they have cats, and despite them promising they'll lock the cats up, the dander is still everywhere and you're horribly allergic, I don't have any Benadryl and I'd rather avoid an after-hours call to the pediatrician because your face has turned into a strawberry with eyeballs." Sometimes a simple explanation will do.

There isn't one particular order you have to do these steps in. It is also a matter of preference. My husband prefers his parenting order of operations to be "I ask, you do, we chat." I tend to do "I ask, we chat, you do." (We'll talk about complementary parenting styles toward the end of the book, don't worry.) Neither of those is wrong and neither of those is right. Ultimately we are still equipping our kids with our reasoning behind our "no" and planting those logical assessment skills in their gray matter.

Here feels like a good place to mention that you can get sick of saying "no." Especially if you are a single parent, solo parent (your partner travels often), or a home-based parent. Decision fatigue is real. And "no" burnout often accompanies it. We can absolutely get sick of being the bad guy when we are the ones constantly telling our kids "no." Even if our decision is sound, well-considered, and for their safety, it gets really annoying and kind of pricks at our emotions to constantly disappoint them. Yeah, they are disappointed that they can't see if they can turn a bed sheet into a parachute by pitching themselves off the roof but we can only hear "Uuuuuugh, Mooooom. That's so unfaaaaair!" so many times before we begin questioning if we have turned into a mean parent.

In my experience there are two ways to counter this "no" burnout. (1) If the risk of injury, property damage, or emotional distress is low, let them but with a cautionary warning. Point out that you don't think it's a good idea, what the potential consequences of this choice could be, and that if they push ahead they are subject to dealing with the fallout with minimal involvement from you. (2) Have a yes day. Set the boundaries of what absolutely cannot be allowed and then commit to saying yes. McDonald's for lunch? Yes. TV till bed? Yes. Outside, if weather is safe to do so? Yes.

My mom pulled that first one on me. I was about twelve or so and in sixth grade when I was absolutely emotionally flattened by failing to abide by boundaries I was allowed to set for myself. At the dawn of my middle school career, I was faced with the biggest choice of my life. I had two opportunities before me and could not choose both. First, I was given a lead role in a local play. It had a ton of speaking lines and a whole solo. As the budding little theater kid, it felt like a once in a lifetime opportunity to play Krista Knowswell in the local production of *Good News!* I gleefully accepted and rehearsals began. (No, there is absolutely no reason you have ever heard of this play. It was a local theater group, not a good local theater group.)

But two weeks after the cast list was posted things got complicated. The kids in the gifted and talented program at my school were going to be competing in a can sculpture contest at the mall. (The fancy mall on the rich side of town too! It even had a Claire's *and* a Hot Topic.) We were going to be spending a weekend wrapping donated canned goods in bits of construction paper and stacking them carefully to create a tiger face. Afterward all the canned goods would be donated to the area food pantry.

The problem was that both the can sculpture competition and the performance were scheduled for the same weekend. If I wanted to play Krista Knowswell I wouldn't be able to go to the can sculpture competition and vice versa. I had to make a choice. My mom pointed out that while the can sculpture thing sounded pretty fun, I had already accepted and committed to the role and had been rehearsing for two weeks. With only one week until the show, it wouldn't be very fair of me to ask them to replace me, only leaving a few days for my replacement to learn all those lines and a whole solo. It was a boundary set by accepting the role and if I chose to walk away from the play, then I would have to deal with any fallout.

But the call of the can siren was too strong. I opted to sign up for the can sculpture competition and let the director know that I would not be performing in *Good News!* She understood and I gleefully began clearing the back of my mother's pantry for canned goods to begin wrapping up in orange, black, and white construction-paper slips.

And then the worst bit came. Friday afternoon before we were to arrive at the fancy mall with boxes and boxes of canned goods ready for the stacking, our principal called all twelve kids on the can sculpture team into her office. The mall had had an issue with an electrical something or other and the whole stage area where we were supposed to be assembling a six-foot tiger face with canned goods had been jackhammered open, chasing a faulty wire. The can sculpture contest was canceled. We were all upset of course, but I had a fallback. All was not lost for little Gwenna.

Or so I thought. When I got home I informed my mom that I would in fact be able to play Krista Knowswell in *Good News!* She promptly disabused me of this notion and reminded me of my self-set boundary. "No, you will not. You decided to give up the role to do the can sculpture. And I'm sorry it got canceled but you're not going to take away that other girl's chance to play Krista because you are free again. You drew a line in the sand, crossed it, and while it didn't go your way, you can't go back the other way."

I was devastated. No canned tiger face. No belting a song chock-full of forced half rhymes and excruciatingly constructed news anchor puns. No nothing. I went from two of the coolest things I'd ever been offered the chance to do to having absolutely no cool things planned for that particular weekend. The fallout fell hard.

Luckily the play director was a kind soul and allowed me to be in the play, not as Krista Knowswell but as a part of the chorus. No lines, no solos, but since I was tall for my age I did get to do a sick move during one of the dance numbers that involved picking up a smaller child and swinging her across the stage to the waiting arms of another chorus member. It wasn't the lead role but it was something.

My mom had disagreed with my decision but rather than tell me, she let me deal with the fallout. She let me choke down that hard-to-swallow pill. She might have been able to advocate for me and get me my part back but she knew I needed to learn this lesson. And learn it I did.

One final note on your ability to define your boundaries, explain yourself, and tell your kid "no." If you find yourself in an emergency situation and need to move, motivate, or hip-check your child out of a dangerous situation, you don't have to pause and explain, "Sweetie, I'm going to shove you really hard and you might fall down and it might hurt because that bus is out of control and veering toward us at a frightening speed." Nope, you can just shove your kid out of the way and explain yourself later. Assuming you need to; sometimes the reasoning for a decision makes itself evident in the fallout of your decision to not allow them to be pancaked by a bus.

To summarize, you can tell your kid "no." The difference between a responsive parent and a non-responsive parent saying "no" is ours is accompanied by an explanation as to why we made the choice to say "no."

See, I told you this was a nice, empowering chapter. Okay, good feels done. Now let's discuss your child saying no right back to you. Brace yourself, bestie.

TL;DR

You can and absolutely should tell your child "no." Responsive parenting is not permissive parenting. The trick to telling your kid "no" responsively is to provide context. You can't always explain yourself at the exact point you have to say "no" but hopefully you can find time to explain yourself later. Sometimes you have to act to enforce the "no." And that's okay. You may disappoint or even upset your child when telling them "no." This is also okay. Gwenna was a part of some really low-budget community theater at some point in her life.

NO: PART II

S o we've established that you can, in fact, safely and respectfully tell your kids "no." Feel better about that? More confident? A little less confused? Excellent. Let me burst a bubble.

What was your child's first word? Take a moment. Recall. Enjoy that little serotonin boost. However, I'd bet that one of your child's first ten words was probably "no." And from the moment they learned it, it was one of the first words to stop being cute. Because once they learn it, they don't stop saying it. Phonetically speaking, it's a very easy word to use and pretty simple to understand what it means and the impact it has.

We know that children learn their first flush of communication skills through emulation. Bitty babies as young as a few months old will mimic their parents' facial expressions and noises. Their first words are often copycatting sounds they hear their parents and caregivers make.

Nearly every parent has a horror story of the time their

precious sentient meatloaf repeated something horribly embarrassing they overheard to a room full of people. I'll save my children the secondhand embarrassment of resharing one of their more colorful copied moments and share one from my own childhood. I don't actually recall doing this, as it happened well before my memories pick up, but my mom made damn sure I got to keep this memory.

When my parents were still married, my mom did not prefer my dad's stubble. He rocked the *Magnum P.I.* mustache like a champ (hello, elder millennial and Gen X readers, I see you), but she would tease him when it had been a bit since he shaved the rest of his face. Remember, he was also an aviation mechanic. So when he'd come home with his five-o'clock shadow, still vaguely covered in mystery mechanic fluids, he'd lean in to give her a kiss on the cheek. My mom would playfully push him away saying, "No, you're a filthy, dirty old man. Get away from me!" It was all in jest. But four-ish-year-old me did not know that.

Fast-forward some unknown amount of time and my mother and I were invited by a friend to their church service. This particular church service included a brief "children's sermon" wherein all the children in the congregation were invited to the front of the stage and the pastor would sit with them and give a little kid–geared mini sermon. When they called for the kids to come forward I gleefully bounced over and sat down. It just so happened this very kind, older preacher with a neatly trimmed beard sat down right next to me. He spoke for a bit while I stared intently at his face.

My mom thought I was paying attention. I was not, apparently. I was plotting. For reasons unknown to any parent, this man asked a question and put a microphone in front of children's faces to give answers. I don't know what he asked and my mother doesn't remember. But he leaned in close and put the microphone in front of my face. Reportedly I looked at him and then the mic and then him before proclaiming, "No! You're a filthy, dirty old man. Get away from me!" My little brain had decided that facial hair equaled filthy, dirty old man because the only time my mom called my dad that was when he needed a shave and was covered in airplane goo from work.

I don't know how my mom found the courage to stay in her seat and not run screaming into the Oklahoma summer heat but she stayed, absolutely mortified. She didn't lecture me. I wasn't in trouble. But she never called my dad a filthy, dirty old man in my presence ever again because her tiny tape recorder (wow, that's a more dated reference than I'd like it to be) would surely make it an issue again.

So yeah, kids parrot their parents. And as you readily employ the magical and empowering "no," your kids are gonna do the same. For a short while, those little baby "nos" will just be sounds. But they figure out pretty quickly how to actually apply them. There was a period where my eldest's favorite word was "no." Not because she always meant "no," but I think because it was just a fun word. I offered to take her three-year-old self to get an ice cream once and she said "no" as she sat down to put on her shoes, practically vibrating with anticipation. When we arrived at this ice creamery, I asked her if she wanted chocolate. She said "no." When I handed her the chocolate ice cream cone I asked if she was excited. She said "no" before excitedly mashing the ice cream into her face. I asked if she liked it. Wanna guess what she said? Amazing deduction powers. She said "no" as she set about downing the whole thing.

She wasn't so much as telling me "no" as she was emulating my near constant string of "no" she heard as a fearless toddler. And that's okay. Remember, we want our children to learn how to establish their own boundaries. "No" is a powerful boundary for a tiny, developing brain to learn.

Great. That's excellent. Wonderful philosophy, you say. Fan-fucking-tastic. They can draw their own boundaries with "no." But they are also screaming "no" at me when I'm trying to remove the poop-filled bag from their bottom or asking that they intake basic nutrition. This is not a fun boundary. I don't like it and cannot respect it.

This is true and the brutal reality of most parenting. The idea that "no" is their first self-set boundary is nice and not false. But also kids suck at understanding their needs. They are often guided more by impulse than considerate thought. So when your kid is setting a boundary you cannot abide by, what do you do?

There is a lot of discussion about children and early lessons in consent. There's no such thing as too young to teach consent. "No" is important. In our family we defined "no" even more specifically for the littles. "No" means "stop and listen." If "no" is their first experiment in autonomy, it's important for parents to respect that, right? Yeah. And also, no. (See what I did there?)

I approach it this way. If I can take "no" for an answer, I'll ask the question. Do you want ketchup with dinner? (That answer has never, ever been "no.") Do you need to go potty? Do you want to go with me to the store? However, if "no" is not an answer I can accept, I don't ask the question in such a way that allows them to establish a boundary I'll have no choice but to cross. Rather than ask my oniony-smelling children if they want a bath I'll ask if they want a colored bath or a bubble bath. I've never asked permission to change a diaper because I don't really care if this is an inconvenient time. I cannot allow you to sit in your own waste product, tiny human.

That doesn't mean I don't respect the boundaries they are able to set for themselves. It means kids are really terrible at balancing their needs with their wants.

One boundary we are incredibly sensitive to is hugging, physical displays of affection, and touch-based play (that's fancy speak for tickling and wrestling). If you don't wanna hug Grandma, you don't have to. Kisses are not required and you damn sure gotta ask people other than Mom and Dad to give kisses. Tickling games are fun but a "no," even one that feels like they didn't mean it, results in the tickles stopping immediately. We won't keep going with the tickle game until the kids tell us "okay, go." Which, in and of itself, the stop-go tickle game has become its own thing. This is the earliest and first version of consent. "No" means stop and listen. There's no such thing as a "no" that doesn't count when it comes to their body and their personal space.

It is important to remind them of that, especially mid-game. If they say "no" and you stop tickling or wrestling or blowing raspberries on their belly, pause for a moment and remind them. "You said 'no' so I stopped. Do you want me to stop altogether or do you just need a breather?" The more you can reinforce that their "no" holds power, even as a very tiny human, the more you're preparing them to hold their own boundary when it isn't a parent, caregiver, or person who loves and respects them unconditionally.

Consent is cool. "No" means stop and listen. Okay, got it.

But what about when they are saying "no" to other stuff like chores, school, homework, or shit that just needs to get done? Is that consent I have to respect?

Nope. Again, kids don't have that little logic voice in their brains, the prefrontal cortex, until their early to mid-twenties. So they are guided by both impulse and parents or caregivers. Remember, "no" means stop and listen. So stop and listen. You might have to guide that explanation out of them but listen all the same. Why are they saying "no"? What's the hang-up, the frustration, the fear, the distaste that's prompting their big fat "no"!?

There may be a valid reason they weren't fully able to verbalize or conceptualize back there. They don't want to do their homework. Okay, why the "no" on the homework? Is it boring and repetitive because they already understand and/or have mastered the concept? That's a valid reason for not wanting to do it. On the other side, are they hopelessly lost and struggling to find even the right questions to ask to better understand the concept? Also a super valid reason for not wanting to do the homework. Neither reason means they don't have to do it, but it will help you, their parent or caregiver, tackle the homework dilemma from a new angle.

Okay, so you do the work, figure out why they are saying "no," and it turns out the whole thing is they "just don't wanna." For them it's a valid reason, but again, it probably doesn't dismiss that they still need to shower regularly or bring their used bowls out of the hellmouth that is their room. That's when you get to reinforce your own boundary with consequences. They can say "no," they can mean "no." But as the parent with the full-functioning brain, you may need to override that "no."

Look, I'm not saying parenting isn't weird, confusing, and downright paradoxical sometimes. Teach them consent but also ignore their "no" if that absolutely is not an answer you can respect. That's an oversimplification, but you get it. Here's where normally the author gives you some excessively researched reason why you can teach consent and also ignore their self-set boundaries sometimes. I am not that author. I'm gonna leave you here with the knowledge that sometimes both of the following can be true.

Kids have a right to say "no."

Parents have a right to determine that their kids' "no" is unacceptable and we still have to do the thing, even in the wake of objections. (This especially applies to hygiene, healthy, safety, and schooling.)

Now we press on to what to do when that "no" your kid tossed at you isn't one you can accept: consequences.

FIELD GUIDE ENTRY: *Weaponized Incompetence*

I've said it before and I'll say it again, kids suck at peopling. That's not really a critique more than it is a statement of fact. It's actually kind of reasonable that kids suck at peopling. Humans are born knowing pretty much nothing and have to learn everything else. And that learning curve is going to be filled with mistakes, errors, and logical disconnects on the regular.

Kids, even those trying their best, have an uncanny knack for finding the hardest, most illogical way to do stuff. More often than we like to recall, kids take a task that to our adult brain seems pretty straightforward, and find the strangest, most difficult way to complete said task. And it is fucking frustrating from time to time.

By its strictest definition, this is because our children are in-competent. You can't know how to do a thing until you learn how to do a thing. We rarely call our children incompetent because it feels like a mean and diminishing word. But if we are looking at it purely by dictionary definition, yeah, kids are incompetent. And that's okay. Most of us go into this whole parenting thing knowing that our children have a lot to learn from us before they are ready to spread their wings and fly out of the nest.

Where it gets tricky is when we get into the muddy waters of weaponized incompetence. It can sometimes feel like your kid is *intentionally* fucking with you. And they might be. But chances are pretty great that your spawn is not doing something the hardest way possible just to vex you. They are incompetent because anyone still learning something is some level of incompetent. That doesn't mean they are necessarily incapable of learning the thing, it means they are still in the process of learning it. This is especially true with regard to kids.

Here's the thing about weaponized incompetence. Weaponized incompetence is the act of intentionally doing something incorrectly or purposefully misunderstanding the instructions in an effort to avoid the activity. Basically, it's pretending to be incompetent so someone else will do something for you. The word "weaponized" really shifts perspective. The minute you weaponize your incompetence, either by pretending you don't know how to complete or figure out a task or outright refusing to learn, you are doing so maliciously. It is either a selfish action because you really hate doing the dishes so you pretend you simply can't do it correctly so a partner, spouse, or roommate just takes the task away from you. Or it is a method of subversive control; you don't feel like you should have to do this chore so you refuse to learn how a lawn mower operates so you can always claim that yard maintenance is outside your skill set, forcing someone else to address the problem.

It's rare that kids are trying to maliciously avoid things. I'm not saying they don't try to avoid things, but for the most part, it isn't malicious. Again, you can't know a thing until you learn a thing. Legitimately not knowing how to do a thing and making consistent mistakes is how we learn.

Okay, but Gwenna, one time my kid stopped in the middle of raking the leaves having apparently forgotten how to do the thing he was doing literally three seconds ago? You're telling me that's not weaponized incompetence?

I'm saying it might not be weaponized incompetence. Because you know what else kids suck at? Communication. Yeah, they are still learning that as well. A nine-year-old who has been tying their shoes for years but all of a sudden can't and wants a parent to do it for them could be just trying to get out of dealing with all those pesky bunnies running round the tree. Or it could be there's a problem there they aren't sure how to define or communicate. Maybe they've outgrown their shoes just enough to make them uncomfortable and they get it into their heads that maybe it's how they are tying them. Maybe the shoelaces need to be replaced.

In my personal experience, I did the shoe-tying trick on my mom. I was ten years old and still using the double bunny ears method. Two loops, crisscross, tuck and pull. A kid in my class had learned a different method and began teasing me for tying my shoes "like a baby." I took it personally. And I stopped wanting to tie my shoes lest someone tease me about it. Since I didn't know how to tie them "like a big kid" I simply stopped trying and requested adult help. They figured out the gig pretty quick and my mom taught me the one-loop method. My sudden inability to tie shoes was not weaponized incompetence, it was a communication gap.

Your forgetful leaf raker might be tired, they might have a blister forming, they might be feeling the effects of dehydration, or they might just be bored. So if they feign not knowing how to do a thing, they get to stop. Again, this isn't weaponized incompetence in my eyes. It is trying to get out of doing something but not maliciously. They aren't trying to make someone else take over their chore or task. They just want to not do it but suck at communicating the reason why.

If you can sort out why they have all of a sudden forgotten a thing they've known for years, you better equip them both with communication skills and perhaps a bit of work ethic. Yep, leaf raking is boring. But it's how we contribute to the house we all share.

TL;DR

Just like you can and should tell your kids "no," your kids can and should tell you "no." "No" is one of the first words kids learn to use and they need to learn that their "no" matters pretty young. There is no such thing as too young to learn consent. "No" means stop and listen. That said, kids have a right to say "no." Parents have a right to determine that "no" is incorrect and we still have to do the thing.

· 13 ·

WELL, IF IT ISN'T THE CONSEQUENCES OF MY OWN ACTIONS

My son might be the world's slowest eater. Now, I'll give him this. He's a good eater and I have to stop and acknowledge the fates here. He eats and while he's got his preferences, he isn't a four-food-only feeder. But he takes fucking forever to get the food down his gullet. The number of meals he has finished in the van because we ran out of time so we popped it all in a baggy to finish on the way might actually outnumber the meals he has finished at mealtime.

There is often some up and down. Inevitably, a morsel of food hits his esophagus and his bladder is like, "Hold up! Lemme drain!" So within the first five minutes of a meal we get "I gotta pee!" This is regardless of whether we sit him on the potty pre-meal or not. Then there are the inevitable escaping blueberries, forks that fought gravity and lost, and the occasional "I remember I am wearing socks and need to look at them immediately" moments. He eats but not without near constant motivation and reminders to do so.

Some meals are better than others, depending on how hungry, tired, and/or stimulated he is when mealtime arrives. One such up/down dinner culminated in what I call a silent movie moment. A silent movie moment is one wherein you can see the whole scene playing out in slow motion in your head the moment before it happens. Most often this results in you being super prophetic about your kids injuring themselves ("Don't run in the driveway, you're going to fa—") as they face-plant in the gravel. "Watch where you step, there's dog shi—" as they put a whole bare foot in a puppy present.

The boy-child accidentally dropped his fork and climbed down off the chair to fetch it. (Our five-second rule is very, very generous. If it didn't spend the night down there, pick it up, wipe it off, and continue. Judge me if you want, but I've had to routinely ask my children to not outright lick the floor. Six of one, half a dozen of another.) As he was climbing back up, I was struck with visions of peas, carrots, and ketchup-coated chicken fries flying through the air like some weird food-based trapeze act. "Buddy, watch out for your plate. Don't spi—" And in that moment as that sentence was leaving my mouth his little hand landed on the edge of the plate. It turned into the world's best food catapult and my vision very much came true. Arching across my kitchen was my son's whole dinner. Every bite of food participated in the culinary circus act.

He was pissed. And I was pissed. Ketchup has a really impressive reach when flung, and my college-educated self had decided white cabinets were the way to go with young children in the house. Now I have white cabinets with very faint pinky-orange polka dots in one specific spot near the dishwasher.

I'm not gonna lie. Between my emotions getting really high and my adult logic brain screaming "How did he not see the plate?!" almost every fiber of my being begged to lose its shit. I even took a big inhale to start yelling at both the inconvenience and the child. But there was one. One single fiber that was like, nope, and that bish was carbon-fiber-spider-web-level strong. Ultimately it was an accident, an accident I've committed as an adult. He didn't do anything wrong. Sure, almost all accidents are "technically" avoidable but seeing as I had straight-up poured coffee down my front earlier that day, I was in no position to preach from the "situational awareness" pulpit.

But as I opened my mouth to let my frustration out, my son started crying. Big, very real tears fell as his frustration bubbled up faster than mine could. He wasn't afraid of getting in trouble. He was very distraught that he believed his dinner was a goner. In that moment, I remembered I didn't have to dole out consequences for his inattentiveness. Sometimes life does that for you. They are called natural consequences.

By the way, I did comfort the boy-child and did not lose my shit. He cleaned up much of the mess while I fixed him a new plate of dinner. I may or may not have rescued some of that chicken from the floor but all the same, he got his plate and was far more careful when he climbed back in the chair that time.

Okay, but wait. Back up. What are natural consequences? Excellent question. I'm going to give you the worst possible definition. Which will actually be the most useful definition. Confused? Perfect. Keep reading.

NATURAL CONSEQUENCES

Natural consequences are what happen when karma gets her way, gravity functions as expected, and/or science continues to work. Your kid ate half a bucket of Halloween candy and now has a tummy ache? The tummy ache is the natural consequence of too much candy at once. Why? 'Cuz biology. Your child raged at a shark game and broke the tablet screen? The broken tablet screen and inevitable loss of the tablet are the natural consequence of mishandled frustration. Why? 'Cuz physics. Your kid consistently forgot to bring home the book fair flyer and now has no money to buy overpriced pencils at the book fair? The despair that is not having a troll-head-topped pencil is the natural consequence of forgetting that flier. Why? 'Cuz time.

Natural consequences are perfect because they make karma, physics, biology, or time the meanie-head, not you. It's also how we learn from mistakes as adults. We encounter more natural consequences than anything else. Hit the snooze button one too many times and the natural consequence is that we either feel rushed or are straight-up late. Ignore the little blinking warning light on our dashboard and the natural consequence is that at some point, likely the most inconvenient point, our car will break down.

For the responsive parent, we want to allow natural consequences to do our dirty work as often as possible. Natural consequences are the perfect balance between form and function. They are the direct explanation of cause and effect. You did this, which caused that, the effect of which is felt now. We don't have to be the villain, although our children won't always agree with this viewpoint, but we get to allow our children to cope with the fallout of their decision-making, their compulsive action, or their lack of consideration/planning/listening ears.

More important, we get to be right there as our children deal with the consequences. Because we can point to gravity or biology or time and say, "This is what happens when . . . ," we aren't the judge, jury, or executioner here. We, as parents, are now in the position of rehab, recovery, and reset guide. We can help them understand how their actions led to the natural consequence, how to avoid repeating this in the future, and begin to offer guidance on how to cope with the loss of opportunity, item, or feeling.

All that said, sometimes we cannot wait on natural consequences. Sometimes we have to be proactive. The opposite of natural consequences are actionable consequences.

ACTIONABLE CONSEQUENCES

Actionable consequences are the consequences we have to dole out in order to prevent injury, reduce harm, or keep our kid pointed in the right direction of becoming a happy, healthy, stable adult.

"If you keep playing with your tablet like that, the screen will break and you won't have a tablet."

versus

"I can't let you keep playing with your tablet like that. If you break the screen we won't have a tablet. So you can switch to a different game that won't make you mad or you can put the tablet away for a while."

The natural consequence of a broken tablet might be what
you choose. But it's more likely that you'll want to save yourself
both the hassle and cost of repairing or replacing that tablet.
So you opt for the actionable consequence that mitigates the
potential damage.

Here is a scenario in which a natural consequence and an actionable consequence are possible.

Your kid is playing on the playground and has climbed to the
very top of the apparatus. I'm talking not just the top of the climbing wall, but sitting on the top of the big support bar that holds
the whole playground up. It's not a spot designed to be played
on. You decide to call out to them and remind them that gravity
exists and their fleshy meat sack is pretty damn breakable.

The natural consequence of playing in a spot not designed
to be played in is falling and hurting themself. That will most
certainly teach them not to climb up there for at least the
foreseeable future. Or at least as long as that cast has to stay
on their arm. But in this case, I'd opt for an actionable consequence. For me that would look something like this.

"Dude, you've made an unsafe choice. I'm going to help you
down from there. No, you may not do it by yourself. You've
kid-bossed too close to the sun, kiddo, and if you fall you could
get seriously hurt. If you climb back up there again, it will be
time to go home."

Ultimately, yes, I want them to remember that climbing ten
feet off the ground on something not designed to be climbed is
a dangerous decision. But allowing the natural consequence to
play out is equally as dangerous. In this case the actionable consequence is twofold. (1) They have to get down and they have
to have help to ensure they do so safely. (2) A further conse-

quence is promised if their impulse control gets the better of them. "We'll go home if you can't stop yourself from spider-monkeying up the architecture."

At its basest level, a consequence is the direct result of an action or choice. Eat ice cream too fast = brain freeze. Get caught speeding = get a ticket. In theory, consequences can help us remember to make a better choice the next time we find ourselves in a similar situation. They don't always help. I know damn well what happens when I eat cheese. I'm still gonna eat cheese. Consequences be damned. On the flip side I let my dogs outside when I thought I smelled skunk just the one time, before I learned to double- and triple-check. The consequence that helped really solidify that lesson was having to buy a new couch. Because when the dogs came inside, freshly sprayed, they jumped straight on the couch. Turns out you cannot remove skunk smell from a couch. At least I can't.

When we are helping our children understand consequences, we are hoping they associate the consequence with the choices that led to it. But seeing as I am rapidly approaching forty years old at the time I write this and still struggle to remember this lesson, give yourself some grace as you continue to ponder exactly how to dole out consequences.

As responsive parents, yes, there are consequences for undesirable or dangerous behavior. Responsive parenting is not permissive parenting. My responsively parented children have definitely been denied activities, requests, or opportunities. Sometimes as a consequence of their actions, sometimes as a natural result of their choices. But consequences were dealt with all the same.

When you tell your child "no" you have the opportunity to describe the consequences.

FIELD ENTRY GUIDE: *Emergency Prevention*

My daughter hated having long hair because of traffic. Yeah, that is a complete and intentional sentence. Allow me to elaborate.

My daughter was about seven and she had hair about down to the middle of her back. It was always braided or pulled back. We were getting out of the car at a busy shopping center one afternoon while she was excitedly describing every pixelated detail of a new *Minecraft* update as she climbed out of the back seat of my PT Cruiser. I dipped back in to grab my phone from the console while she continued to chatter. When I stood back up she was absently wandering into the driving lane of the parking lot with a rather large, absently driven pickup truck headed right for her.

I reached out and grasped the only thing I could get my hands on, her ponytail, and yanked her back. In doing so, not only did I save her from being pancaked by a King Ranch edition manmobile, I ripped out a not insignificant chunk of her hair that had been wrapped too tightly in the hair band near the nape of her neck. She started crying out of fear and pain. I started crying out of fear and guilt. And there we sat, in the parking lot in front of a home decor store, crying.

Was there a better way to handle that? Probably. Could I have thought of it before taking an ambulance ride with my seriously injured offspring? Unlikely. When we as parents find ourselves in emergency or potentially emergency situations, it's still okay to react rather than respond. I'm aware that feels like a weird thing to say in a book about responsive parenting. Doesn't make it less true. Kids have terrible situational awareness and will absolutely walk into traffic without noticing the danger. Or, depending on the age of your child, without even understanding it's dangerous. It's easier and preferable to apologize for scaring or hurting them than to let the scenario play out. Because the fear and/or pain you cause in preventing an accident will almost surely be less than the actual accident.

While I have you here, please remember that you are human. If you turn to see your kid endangering themselves and you banshee screech at them, lose your temper, or do something that sane, considered, regulated you would never, ever do, that's okay. It really, really is. Situations wherein we find our children in danger are stressful. Stress makes cortisol and adrenaline in the brain. It's really hard for cortisol to be level when our brains are flooded with it. Adrenaline makes us feel the effects of stress in a physical way.

Again, apologies are just as useful as calm communication when raising tiny humans. Give yourself some grace if you lost your shit as your child's life flashed before your eyes.

TL;DR

Just like boundaries, consequences are a required part of responsive parenting. The best consequences are directly related to the boundary that was crossed or rule broken. There are two types of consequences to choose from. Natural consequence: You left the tablet on the floor, stepped on it, broke it, and now you don't have a tablet. Actionable consequence: You left the tablet on the floor, so I took it away to prevent you from stepping on it and breaking it. You still don't have a tablet but now no one has to pay for it to be repaired or replaced.

14

DEVELOPMENTALLY APPROPRIATE IS JUST CODE FOR "THIS TOO SHALL PASS"

his far into the book, if there's anything you should be able to take away from it by now it's this: Responsive parenting won't stop your children from acting like children. It simply adjusts how you respond to their behavior, good, bad, or otherwise. Any sort of intentional parenting style carries with it this narrative that if you parent well, your children will never manifest the demons of "bad behavior." Nope. Your precious angels have within them the makings of hellbeasts.

Childhood is an amalgamation of changes. Nothing but changes: physical, mental, emotional. Stuff doesn't stop changing from the moment they are born until the moment they move out. (And really even after that: Life is either change or the lack thereof.) How those changes manifest will vary wildly, however. That's code for "yeah, they are gonna do weird shit."

I can't tell you exactly what. I just know it's going to be weird. This generates a bunch of behaviors that are lumped in one big, frustrating category of "developmentally appropriate." Just go ahead and assume for the remainder of this chapter if I say something that makes you feel less than enthusiastic, I am also muttering an apologetic encouragement. That will save a whole bunch of "sorrys" after most of the paragraphs to follow.

Disclaimer: If you don't have a toddler as you read this, you are going to be really tempted to skip this chapter. Don't. There's some stuff in here for you parents of older children too, even if it's just basking in the utter relief that you don't have to parent toddlers anymore. But seriously, I'm gonna talk about more than toddlers here in just a second. Stick with me.

I don't remember being a toddler. But I vividly remember raising them. I have to believe that being a toddler is simultaneously the best and the worst. Everything is new and exciting. Everything is big. Sometimes too big and that's frustrating and often scary. They can go pretty much everywhere now that they are walking but there is a frustratingly high number of gates, locks, plastic doodads, and cobbled-together toddler-proofing thingies that lock down the coolest stuff. The food is either magical or poison, no in-between. Toddlers are finally able to express all those emotions they feel in ways other than giggling or screaming. Now they can also nod, point, pinch, bite, hit, kick, head bang, throw shit, hold their breath till they pass out, rage-vomit, and destroy things. Cool.

What they cannot do is figure out how to make these fucking adults understand that they just want a goddamn applesauce. Language is developing. Slowly. Too slowly. As a mother, I often wished there were just a Matrix-style upload of language. Just "Okay, we've made it eighteen months, the baby sign is cute and all but speaking is better. Here, let me just upload the English module here." But that's not how it works. And here we are elbow deep in a field guide for how to survive this bit.

The following is either going to be wildly encouraging or deeply disappointing. Toddlers are universally assholes. Your vampiric twenty-month-old is not unique in his incredible ability to sink his teeth into human flesh at the slightest hint of disappointment. Most things we view as the most assholish behaviors in toddlers are—say it with me now—"developmentally appropriate." Essentially that's the fancy way of saying yep, it's annoying, but they'll grow out of it.

Now that doesn't mean that you need to invest in full-body armor, nor do you just have to take it. You can do some stuff to deter, distract, encourage more desirable reactions to being pissed off, and prime the pathway of emotional understanding.

But yeah, for the most part, it's just a waiting game. As your future soccer star grows, she'll develop more language, get a better bead on her feelings, master a few coping skills, and quit attempting to penalty-kick your shins every time she doesn't get her way. (Sorry. I know I said I wasn't going to apologize again but that one hurt to type. It had to hurt more to read if you're in the thick of it.)

"Awesome," says you, the exhausted and frustrated parent wrangling a toddler-shaped anger goblin. "You said I didn't have to just take it. So, what do I do?"

I proudly present to you the most lackluster quasi-solution to fit throwing. The three Rs: reinforce, redirect, repeat. It is an imperfect solution to the absolute dumpster fire that are the emotions pouring out of your toddler's underdeveloped brain. But it's something. We discussed this just a little bit in the Big Feels Loop-De-Loo chapter but it deserves a deeper dive.

Let's take a scenario that most parents have probably experienced. Your child is mad for a really inane reason and in the midst of your trying to get them to calm the eff down, they pull that tiny, pudgy arm back and let it sail. You see it coming, that furious little hand extended, but don't have time to react. Instead, you sit stunned with a slight sting on your cheek because your beta-version human hauled off and bitch-slapped you. He stands before you, kinda snotty, red-faced, and likely still screaming like a banshee, completely unfazed that he just coldcocked his parent.

You ignore the instinct to throw hands with a baby. First, you would trounce him utterly and there is no thrill of victory in beating someone an eighth of your size. Second, you've avowed yourself to practice intentional, responsive parenting. Third, your child is throwing a fit over something unchangeable. "Yeah, kid, the sun is up. It's two p.m. That's just how the sun works." If he's struggling to understand the basic night and day cycle, there's little chance of him following a long diatribe about not meeting anger with violence and how that's led to some really fucked-up goings-on throughout the course of history. So, what are you supposed to do? Just let him get away with that? Here come the three *R*s.

> **Reinforce:** "Sir! That is not okay. You hit me and you hurt me. I will not let you hurt me!" Then you gently move him about an arm's length away. Luckily your arms are longer than his so if he's gonna swing again, he won't catch your cheek this time. "You are mad, but hands are not for hitting!"
>
> **Redirect:** "Mommy is going to go get a boo-boo buddy (ice pack—ours is in the shape of a kitty) for her cheek

'cuz it hurts when you get hit. Can you help me? Hold Momma's cup and let's go get a boo-boo buddy." This might feel a touch dramatic but kids are still learning cause and effect. The more times you can sort of drive home the correlated actions of hit = hurt, the quicker they switch to other, less violent attempts at regulating their emotions. There's a reason toddler-targeted shows are over-the-top exaggerated. Kids need that high-energy form of communication to help their little brains make the appropriate associations.

Repeat: Hopefully by now the fit has subsided, the kid is distracted, and it's okay that the sun is still up. And the hitting issue is totally all fixed and will never happen again because you are just a badass at the parenting gig. Nope. It's likely going to happen again. If it's not hitting it could be kicking or biting or face-planting himself on the floor in a full flailing tantrum. And so, you'll repeat this process. And repeat it. And repeat it until you're wholly convinced nothing is going to work and you have born unto this world a serial killer/cannibal.

I did warn you the technique is pretty lackluster. But it is effective—over time. That's the bit that gets us tripped up. Most results of any parenting technique are not immediate. They take time, consistency, and repetition to really set in. In the case of developmentally appropriate behaviors, time is really the biggest factor. The three *R*s give you something to do in the heat of the moment and help you maintain that consistency. That's about it.

FIELD GUIDE ENTRY:
My Kid Is Only an Asshole to Me

So, you get your kid back from school, day care, the sitter, or a friend's house and get nothing but reports that your angel was extra angelic. Cool story, you think, as you mentally prepare yourself for the battlefield that is your home life. The fits, the lashing out, the screaming, the summoning of demons. Why is your kid good for everyone else but seems to hate you especially? Probably because you have a good attachment with them. Your kiddo absolutely melting down the minute they get home is likely something called "post-restraint collapse." Essentially, they've been bottling up the energy all day and once they are safe at home, they gotta let it loose. And they trust you, their parent, to still love them, care for them, and be there once the manic energy is released. Combat this by giving them some decompression time when they walk in the door. Pop on a short show, hand them the tablet, or encourage them to go do a thing they enjoy for X number of minutes before anything else happens. Delay dinner, baths, homework, whatever for a short while to let everyone sort of take a breath, reset, and rest for just a moment.

Gwenna, did you just spend several pages telling me a whole technique that isn't going to actually help . . . it just distracts me from enduring a "developmentally appropriate" behavior that sucks?

I didn't say it doesn't help. It just doesn't feel like it's helping immediately (or at all) while you're in the thick of it. Practicing the three Rs is really like laying a foundation for your kid to better understand and deal with their more complex feelings later. As I mentioned before, if you default to the three Rs, you are being consistent in your response to your kid being a jerk. You're also demonstrating that the lashing out didn't actually get them their way. It didn't reward them with a big reaction or extra attention. Really, it didn't result in much of anything.

In her book *Hunt, Gather, Parent,* Michaeleen Doucleff describes how she traveled to an Inuit village in Canada to learn how the Inuit people have been raising kids for literal centuries. It was there that she was shown the magic of ignoring your kid when they are being jerks. According to Doucleff, in Inuit parenting, bad behavior, tantrums, meltdowns, and lashing out aren't met with any more enthusiasm or energy than day-to-day life requires. A child throwing a fit isn't watched, spoken to, handled, or acknowledged until they get it out of their system and can communicate once more. (Of course, they are supervised, but, like, stealthily.) According to Doucleff, most tantrums were over in moments because the children understood that they could feel their big feel but the big ol' screaming fit wasn't going to accomplish anything.

That's all well and great for the Inuit who have been doing this for generations. If you ignore a child in a tantrum, it could shut the tantrum down. Or it could get the child to escalate. Shifting to a new parenting technique might take practice. But I tried that with my own fit-prone youngest after reading Doucleff's description. My youngest daughter has a bit of a bossy streak and is very protective of her things (to be understood here as anything she thinks is hers, regardless of actual ownership).

It was a regular winter day when my three-year-old stood screaming at me, absolutely distraught that her brother had touched a dinosaur toy she'd set down five minutes ago. (It was his dinosaur toy, mind you.) My instinct was to try to talk her out of the feels, make the screaming stop, and shift focus to something else. But I decided to take a lesson from the Inuit and ignore her. I let my eyes drift away, turned my head away from her slightly, and made my expression as neutral as I could get it. The girl-child snuffled and snarled and wailed for a minute before I heard the telltale sniffle of a kid coming out of a fit. She was calming herself down. *She was calming herself the eff down.* When the screaming wasn't working for her, she gave it up.

Now, that doesn't work every time in our house. Sometimes having a fit ignored makes them double down. But it does work more times than it doesn't.

That's what the first *R,* reinforce, looks like in the long game. Eventually, after constantly showing them this behavior isn't okay, they will stop doing it. Either because they found a better way to communicate their need or because you simply weren't responding to it in the way they'd hoped.

Screaming doesn't help. "I will not let you scream to get your way. Your screaming has no effect on me. I am bored by your screams, tiny human." I wish I were the type of parent who could tell you with carefully charted empirical data that the fit throwing has reduced since finding a successful way to reinforce that screaming doesn't work. But I'm not that organized. I think we have fewer screaming fits. Or maybe I'm just less bothered by them now. Either way feels like a win.

"But what about that redirect? That's definitely just a useless step to make everybody feel better." I mean, you're not wrong. But you're not totally right either. It is a step to make everybody feel better. But it isn't useless. Redirection removes attention from the problem at hand, gives space and time to calm down, and might just show them the problem isn't a problem at all.

With the exception of something that could or has caused bodily harm, injury, or critical property damage, there are very few things that cannot simply be addressed later. Redirecting your kids' attention and energy to something other than whatever pissed them off in the first place is going to give everyone a moment to breathe, process, and assess before addressing.

In the case of toddlers, seven out of ten times the big feeling was spawned by a thing that isn't that big a deal. They were hangry, they lashed out—redirect to a snack. They were tired, they lashed out—redirect to a calmer activity. They were just toddlers, they lashed out—show them something shiny and the big feeling will pass. Lashing out is developmentally appropriate.

In the case of older kids up to teens, the redirect still works. Your kid is pissed off about a perceived social slight at school and taking it out on you. Asking them to engage with something else for just a moment will give both of your brains a moment to chill out. You, if not your kid, will be able to parse out the problem a little better in that moment of redirected energy.

I'm going to be science-y for just a second. Bear with me. The part of the brain that controls most of the big emotions is the amygdala. That is online pretty much from day one. Newborns can feel fear, disgust, and contentment. The part of the brain that helps us decide rational ways to cope with feelings is the prefrontal cortex. That bit doesn't actually fully mature until your early to mid-twenties. So for the better part of two decades, kids are just flailing in the wind on the emotional front. They feel just as deeply as full-grown adults without the little voice inside their heads to bully them out of throwing a full-fledged tantrum in public because of those feelings. Okay, that's less science-y than I thought it was going to be but whatever. You get it.

Back to that enraged teen taking out their emotional turmoil on you. Redirecting a school-ager to teenager isn't any more complex than redirecting an infant. In the midst of their blowup, we find a space to say, "Hey, I want a cookie. Do you want a cookie?" Or potentially "I'm going to step outside with the dog, come with me." The pause as they process outside-the-shitshow information is often enough to force a good deep breath. While fetching said cookie or changing said scenery there is a moment wherein we can engage our prefrontal cortex on their behalf. They are feeling X feeling because of Y factor. A generally acceptable way to handle this is Z.

Essentially you trick them into giving you a hot second so you can brain for them.

And finally, the repeat. This bit sucks the most. You will feel like you're going to lose your cool and potentially explode. That's normal. Because every time you have to rinse and repeat those first two Rs it feels like one step forward, two steps back. But it's not. It's a pattern. It's the foundation. Every time you repeat, they get this method of working through their own problems pushed just a little further into their subconscious. So, when they are presented with a problem sans parental units, they are more likely to default to reinforcing their own emotional validity, understand that a boundary they set has been crossed, how that's wrong, and give themselves permission to step back and assess.

TL;DR

Tiny humans are awful at being people because they are still learning how not to be awful. They are impulsive, uncoordinated, emotional, and unpredictable. A lot of what drives us as parents up a wall in the earliest years of child-rearing is developmentally appropriate. Knowing that all kids do this shit does not make it feel any better. The best way to responsively parent very young children in the infant to toddler stage is (1) Reinforce: Teeth are not for biting; (2) Redirect: Let's go get a silicone chewy for those chompers; and (3) Repeat: And repeat and repeat and repeat. Either it will sink in or they will grow out of it.

15

DISOBEDIENCE, MANIPULATION, AND OTHER GROWN-UP WORDS

'm the first to say I don't like the term "first-time mom." It's deceptive. "First-time mom" is an apt descriptor for a mom trying not to fuck up her first child. I'll concede that. But it leaves out that already having one spawn does not mean you know what you're supposed to be doing with any subsequent crotch goblins. You may have kept one tiny human alive, maybe even thriving, but the minute you add another one to the mix, you're a first-time mom all over again. It's your first time being a mom of two (or three or eight) children. And it's your first time being a mom to those particular beta-version humans. It's a whole new story you're writing.

I'll admit this is a recently held belief for me. It wasn't until my younger children came along that I realized my prior experience with not unaliving your own offspring is not a guarantee you know what to do with the next kid.

My eldest was born with an impeccable sense of justice.

She has always been a stickler for the rules, for understanding how and why things are, and with the fairness of all experiences. She was in second grade when she came home one day absolutely distraught. Her class had been preparing all week for a Quiz Bowl, a trivia-type game that is some weird blend of *Jeopardy!* and *Family Feud*. At first it had seemed that her class was poised to win it. But the day came and went and as she climbed into the car she burst into tears. Her class hadn't just lost. They'd been disqualified. Why? One of the students had cheated and had a review sheet hidden in her pocket. You want to know who turned that student in? My daughter. She told the teacher that her teammate was cheating, knowing full well what the consequences of this confession would be. Didn't ease the sting any but nevertheless she turned in the cheater and got her own team disqualified.

In her earliest years, she was incredibly helpful, empathetic, intuitive, easy to work with. She was the false idol of "motherhood isn't all that hard." I fell victim to this mentality quickly. It's how they get you; the fates, karma, the gods, innate biological need for immortality, whatever you want to blame it on. The first child convinces you to have more.

Then comes the second. All bets off. The universe will hand some of us a compliant, easy, gentle-spirited wonder in our first child. Then it will laugh in our faces as we welcome to the world a creature that was likely a violent sociopath in a previous life.

My son, technically my middle child, is the opposite of my eldest in just about every way. He exists in his own world and while he is very helpful, he is also creative in his interpretation of what actually "helps."

In our home we don't have chores so much as a reasonable

expectation of contribution. When the kids are very tiny, there isn't much expectation. As they grow, the reasonable expectation grows with them. By eighteen months old, I figured they were old enough to contribute to the clean-up process, especially of their own toys. Each night, as part of our bedtime routine, we worked together to clean up their toys, books, and stuffies. Once they got fairly sufficient at helping with that, we added additional clean-up windows whenever we shifted activities or were getting ready to leave the house.

One afternoon when the littles were about two, the girl-child and the husband unit were out at the store. So the boy-child and I were chilling at home when he decided he wanted to play outside.

"Sure, buddy. But we gotta clean up first. You start cleaning up and I'm going to go get the sunscreen."

"K, Momma." Confident and pleased that I'd raised such an intelligent, helpful child, I strutted out to grab the promised lotion. Upon my return I found my toddler halfway up his tall boy dresser, his arm reaching toward the top with a toy garbage truck clutched in his pudgy little hands.

"Dude? Whatcha doin' there, bud?" I asked, wildly confused and attempting to stuff down the "doing dangerous shit" panic that wanted to rise in my chest and make me freak out.

"Up!" my son shouted. He was still preverbal at that point and would later need speech therapy, but my toddlerese was strong. "Up!" he repeated, so proud of himself and his reasonable contribution.

It took me a hot sec to figure out what had transpired. Despite having worked with us to clean up his toys, the boy-child had not associated putting toys away with the phrase "clean up." My best guess of toddler reasoning was that he knew the word "up" meant high; the top of his dresser was the highest point he could reach, thus "clean up" meant put the toys up high.

That's not what I meant at all. But he couldn't have possibly known that. I'd never adequately explained to him what "clean up" meant. At least not in a way he could truly understand. He'd tried to understand. And wasn't that far off if you want to get technical. The toys were no longer scattered. The "clean" part he got. The "up" part lost him.

That wasn't his fault. It wasn't mine. It was just a learning curve that I'd forgotten.

It wasn't until my youngest kids came along that I realized how often I took for granted what kids do and do not understand. Parents share a universal habit of either under- or over-estimating our kids on the regular.

I am quite guilty of applying my adult interpretation to my child's very childish behaviors. I forget that not only are they bad at being people but that it's my job to rectify that. Things like manipulation, disobedience. These are grown-up concepts that children are not born understanding. And they are more nuanced than even grown-ups remember.

I break down the idea of disobedience into five categories. The kids don't care but this helps me assess what's going on. It forces me to take a moment and decide how to move forward with teaching my tiny humans how to people better.

> **Intentional:** I know the boundary. I understand the consequences. I consciously cross the boundary. I decided the reward outweighs the risk.
> **Unintentional:** I didn't know or understand the boundary. I was unclear on the consequences. I accidentally

crossed the boundary. I didn't know I was or was not supposed to do the thing.

Experimental: I know the boundary. I don't understand the consequences. I consciously cross the boundary. I just want to see what happens.

Impulsive: I know the boundary but I forgot. I may know the consequences but they didn't occur to me. I accidentally crossed the boundary. I was acting with little to no forethought.

Malicious: I know the boundary. I understand the consequences. I consciously cross the boundary purely for the sake of crossing the boundary. I'm doing it for the attention or to inspire a negative emotion in someone else.

Please don't assume they outgrow any of these versions of disobedience. Grown adults accidentally break rules all the time. Sometimes it's because they are zoned out and forgot they'd entered a school zone, thus winning themselves a ticket.

And they aren't a bad kid even if they routinely choose intentional disobedience. Again, think of adults and why someone might choose disobedience. An adult rushing to the hospital for a sick loved one might consciously opt to make traffic laws optional. Not because they want to risk others' safety, but because they've decided the rewards outweigh the risks.

Even malicious disobedience can still be for the right reasons. A protester consciously crossing a police line and getting themselves arrested to help make a point, raise awareness, and motivate those left behind is practicing malicious disobedience.

I was eighteen and living with my mother. She had a rule that I could dye my hair but it had to be a natural color, no wild, vivid colors. I abided by that rule begrudgingly, less because of my mother and more because my various extracurricular activities also forbade vibrant hair colors. But the day I graduated high school, I took myself to the beauty supply store and bought a big tub of blue Manic Panic. I slipped into the bathroom and slathered my shoulder-length hair in the glorious blue paste. After processing and rinsing, I proudly and rebelliously stepped into my mother's (still) very brown living room.

She took one look at me, squinted her eyes, and I braced for the onslaught. I'd preplanned this whole argument. This was intentional malicious disobedience in its truest form. My mother opened her mouth. I was ready. Instead of berating me she simply said, "You missed some spots. Go back and hit your roots again."

You know that sound a balloon makes when you stretch the neck out as it deflates? I felt that sound as a physical sensation. I hung my head, disappointed my little blue-tinged rebellion had flopped so incredibly hard. I'd aimed for malicious disobedience. Somehow I landed in "my mom moved the boundary and just hadn't told me." Okay.

Deciding what motivated your child to push a boundary, break a rule, do a thing you expected them to know better than to do can really help you decide how to handle the situation. Depending on what rule was disobeyed and what motivated them to that disobedience, it might be time for a consequence. This would probably (though no rule is absolute) be the case for intentional disobedience. Then again, it might be time to revisit that boundary (we talked about this a couple of chapters back).

They may have earned themselves a natural consequence. You can tell a child until you're blue in the face that the red light means the stove top is hot; don't touch. Some kids simply won't believe you until they touch it. This is experimental disobedience. Seven of ten times they figure out the hard way why that particular boundary existed.

Your kids might need more clarification either on the why, the how, or the parameters of the boundary if you're in unintentional or impulsive disobedience. They might just need a reminder. "Buddy, you can't dart into traffic. The cars will win that game every time." For the 73,923rd time, responsive parenting is not permissive parenting.

"Disobedience" is a grown-up word we apply to kid behavior. But what about other grown-up words like "manipulation"? First we have to ask, are kids manipulative? We give birth to really useless meat sacks with lungs. They have no mobility, dexterity, language. All they have is self-preservation instinct, some super basic automated bodily functions, a full range of emotions but no way to adequately communicate those, and the ability to scream, cry, and make those adorable heart-melting coo sounds. But it isn't manipulation, it's self-preservation. Literally the instinct to survive.

Kids are also wildly impulsive. Somewhere between birth and the ability to walk, I imagine this massive battle erupts in their little brains. How a kid can make sense out of the near constant battle between their self-preservation instinct and their complete and utter lack of impulse control is beyond me. "I'm hungry, tell Mom, she'll feed me," but also "Belly-flopping off the back of this couch onto these shards of glass and flaming coals looks super fun."

The older they get, the more likely they are to tiptoe into manipulation. Adults are wildly guilty of manipulating each other constantly. But kids aren't going to post revenge porn or dox you. They will try to split parents (asking Dad because Mommy said no) and yeah, that could be termed manipulative, but it's probably just more of that poor impulse control.

In order to willfully manipulate you have to master four important concepts.*

- hypothetical thinking
- critical and rational thinking
- empathy
- impulse control

Turns out most kids are really awful at most of those things. The younger they are, the less likely they are to be able to consciously manipulate you. Most of the time they just aren't thinking beyond the here, the now, the temptation, or the desire of the moment. If you feel like your child is consciously manipulating you, you might consider turning that wayward eye inward. You feel manipulated. Valid. But why do you feel that way? Because I'm going to wager your kid isn't capable of actually manipulating you. She might be triggering you. She might be dredging up some long dormant feeling. But she isn't manipulating you. She probably can't.

---

* Olga V. Kozachek. "The Age and the Psychological Conditions of the Manipulative Behavior of Preschool Children." *Journal of Psychology and Clinical Psychiatry* 9, 4 (2018): DOI: 10.15406/jpcpy.2018.09.00548.

FIELD GUIDE ENTRY: *Obedience Vs. Submission*

Responsive parenting is not permissive parenting. You're sick of reading it. I'm never going to be sick of typing it because I'm really gonna need to drive that point home. A constant, and I mean constant, debate encountered anytime responsive (or gentle) parenting is brought up is obedience versus submission. There seems to be a lack of distinction between these two words in the context of parenting.

They are in fact very, very different. It's made worse when you look at the definitions. "Obedience" is defined as the act or practice of obeying, dutiful or submissive compliance; whereas "submission" is an act or instance of submitting, or yielding control to a more powerful or authoritative entity.

As parents we want (and sometimes have to expect) obedience. We've laid out boundaries, expectations, and guidelines designed to keep our chaos goblins safe and plodding along the "growing up to be a decent human" path. Obeying the rules is something we have to do a lot as adults. We obey laws, mind our manners, adhere to many social norms, and can reasonably expect most other adults to do the same. Our job as parents is to equip our children with not just the understanding but the desire to be obedient. Obedience not only keeps us safe but it is an exercise in empathy and respect for others. As long as the rules are clearly explained, reasonably enforced, and applied with logic, most adults don't have a problem obeying.

However, as a responsive parent, we aren't aiming for blind obedience. In some ways, as frustrating as it is, we want our children to question us. We need them to understand *why* a boundary exists as well as what the consequence is for crossing the boundary. Ultimately this is because we want them to be able to identify and call out really poor rules or abuses of power in our absence. So either we explain our rules and expectations from the outset or we allow our children to come at us with a healthy dose of skepticism and questioning.

Submissiveness on the other hand is exactly that, blind obedience. "Because I said so"; "Because I'm a grown-up"; "Because that's just the way it is." These are rather lackluster reasons for any kid to do a thing we've asked, demanded, or commanded. It leaves no room for explanation or exploration. Submissive behaviors in childhood are linked to submissive behaviors in adults. Children who were ruled with fear and intimidation often lack some problem-solving skills later in life. Carolyn Solo, a licensed clinical social worker out of Pennsylvania, specializes in parenting and perinatal mental health and points to studies that support this.[*]

Children who were raised in a fear-based system of submission don't have the opportunity to learn from mistakes. They try to hide mistakes for fear of being disciplined. Mistakes are not viewed as something to learn from but rather to be ashamed of. These kids also tend to have higher instances of mental health issues as adults due to low self-esteem and a lack of regulatory tools.[†]

On the flip side, children who are expected to submit without question are more likely to rebel, potentially dangerously. I'm not talking blue hair dye or surprise belly-button piercings, but swinging for the fences and experimenting with more dangerous rebellious behavior. I'm not saying that if you yelled at your child regularly they are going to recreate the entire plot of *Breaking Bad*. I'm saying the science says rebellious teens and young adults often started out as submissive kids.[‡]

---

[*] Simone Marie. "The Consequences of Fear-Based Parenting and What to Do Instead." *PsychCentral* (April 25, 2022): https://psychcentral.com/blog/discipline-without-fear#what-it-is.

[†] John David Eun et al. "Parenting Style and Mental Disorders in a Nationally Representative Sample of US Adolescents." *Social Psychiatry and Psychiatric Epidemiology* 53, 1 (January 2018): 11–20, https://pubmed.ncbi.nlm.nih.gov/29110024/.

[‡] Al Ubaidi BA (2017) "Cost of Growing up in Dysfunctional Family." J Fam Med Dis Prev 3:059. doi.org/10.23937/2469-5793/1510059

Name a fancy word for a behavior and you can probably redefine it as "acting out." Misbehaving, defiance, manipulation, being difficult—they're all versions of acting out in some sense. We can classify any sort of rule breaking or fit throwing as "acting out" which can be traced to a few different stimuli.

1. There is an unmet need. And honestly, sometimes that unmet need is simple. They are hungry, tired, overstimulated, or all of the above. But honestly, sometimes that need is incorrect. Kids will often confuse need with want. They want a piece of candy. And they want it so hard it feels like a need. Since they are still learning all those fun things like self-control, risk assessment, and not being a jerk, that real or perceived need drives them to act out.

2. A boundary needs to be reassessed. You already read that chapter. Or maybe you didn't, I don't know, but go back a few chapters. There's plenty there about boundaries and how, when, and why you should move them.

3. They were trying to exert independence or self-sufficiency. A kid is just a tiny adult who hasn't learned how to properly person yet. Occasionally they will attempt to solve their own problems. Sometimes out of altruism (they want to help), or emulation (they want to be like their parents/teachers/siblings/older people), or because they couldn't readily come to another solution. Why is there a full gallon of milk all over the kitchen? Because they

tried to pour it on their own cereal in an attempt to meet their own needs.

4. They simply don't know what they are doing because they haven't learned it yet. A three-year-old making banshee screeches in the car could absolutely make driving way harder than it needs to be. But there is no reason for her to know that banshee screeches in the car make driving a potentially hazardous endeavor. You'll have to teach her that. And then teach it to her again the next time you're in the car because toddlers have the memory of a goldfish. 'Cuz science, but the effect is the same.

5. They suck at risk assessment. Again with the impulse control. Occasionally I'm tempted to look at my children and just scream, "Fucking why? Why would it occur to anyone on the planet to shove thirty-two paper clips up their nose?" But they don't know the answer to that. And they certainly didn't pause to ask themselves what happens *after* they shove thirty-two paper clips up their nose. The thought occurred to them, the opportunity presented itself, and I guess we're going to the godforsaken urgent care. Get in the damn van.

Now this is not to say that children cannot act out maliciously. Some children can be vengeful in the wake of a fit. Older children and teens can definitely willfully manipulate or at least attempt to manipulate their parents or authority figures. In these cases, you're beyond my expertise and it's time to reach out to one of those specialized professionals like a therapist or psychiatrist. Something is motivating those behaviors and the sooner you can suss that out and begin addressing the core of the issues, the sooner you can look fondly back at them in the rearview mirror.

FIELD GUIDE ENTRY: *Lying*

If there is one thing that will send me straight to a potential red-zone reaction, it's catching my kids in a lie, especially a carefully crafted, premeditated untruth. They weren't just spur of the moment attempting to keep themselves out of trouble, they calculated and formulated and plotted a story designed to slip between the cracks.

However, it's important to note that lying is as old as human communication.* We've been dishonest with each other since we figured out how to vibrate our vocal chords in a controlled fashion. When dealing with our children lying right to our faces, it helps to lump the lies into categories to decide how to react.

There are four very distinct reasons humans are compelled to lie to each other.

1. Avoid responsibility, consequence, or fallout (defensive lies)
2. Protect the feelings or perceived well-being of the person asking (altruistic lies)
3. Conceal a misunderstanding or confusion around an event (protective lies)
4. A feeling of pressure to provide information requested (compelled lies)

With children and some neurodivergent people, I add a fifth category for lies:

---

* Allison Kornet. "The Truth About Lying." *Psychology Today* (May 1, 1997): https://www .psychologytoday.com/us/articles/199705/the-truth-about-lying.

5. A disconnection or altered memory in which they cannot distinguish between fact and fiction (creative lies, absent lies)

Note here I dismiss the very surface-level small-talk-type lies. You can tell me I'm pretty even on days you and I both know I look like hot garbage. I know it's a lie. But I'm not mad. Things like "I'm fine." Or "No, that dress doesn't make your ass look big." If you want to get specific, these are altruistic lies and just a part of being sensitive to the feelings of others. The truth is that dress does look truly awful but if you love it and feel good in it, who am I to tear you down? In this case the "truth" is subjective. My opinion of your dress is true. Your opinion of your dress is true. So I can simply keep my mouth shut and let you enjoy your dress.

When you're faced with a child telling lies right to your face, first regulate. Remember there is almost nothing that needs to be handled immediately so long as life, limb, and property are in no danger of imminent damage. Even if the lie does not have you elevated to the point you need to calm down, you might need to take some time and suss out what type of lie your child is crafting. It might make it easier to decide how to proceed.

In the case of defensive lies, we move straight into consequences. There was already a whole chapter on that one. For altruistic and protective lies, it leads to the discussion that the truth is the best option, even when it's hard or when it might hurt. The lie will always hurt more than the truth in the long run. And for compelled and creative lies, you are gonna have to turn that finger inward.

Your line of questioning, your tone, your emotional regulation, or your communication may have triggered a flight response in your kiddo. And that's not to say I think you are going all FBI interrogation on them. It's just that however you landed there, they felt some sort of pressure they didn't understand or process well. It's not a sign you're parenting poorly. It's a sign that you found a communication glitch between you and your kid. That's okay. Now you know and can try different ways of asking for further clarification or a reason behind a choice they made.

Ways to avoid or at least minimize lying:

1. Don't give them questions that leave the opportunity to lie. If you know without a doubt they have eaten the Oreos, when you approach them, don't give them an out. Instead of opening with "Did you eat the Oreos?" which opens the door for them to deny, try "When you're hungry, what should you do?" Or "When is it okay to get into the Oreos?" This is going to save a whole lot of headache—you're not only addressing the Oreo issue, you're avoiding adding a potential lie into the mix.
2. Don't trap them into feeling like there's only one correct answer. (Avoid compelled or altruistic lies.)
3. Remember that sometimes the truth isn't worth knowing. Especially on little things (even if they feel big at the time). Who broke the lamp might feel important in the moment, but in the grand scheme of things, all the ankle biters in the house could probably help clean it up and discuss a safe place to play games.

TL;DR

Often we are quick to assume that kids understand what they are doing when they break a rule. Sometimes this is true. Sometimes it is not. Disobedience is kind of part of being a kid. Boundaries are important. But for kids, learning how to test, move, and hold their own limits requires pushing or straight-up destroying those boundaries. Kids will and, to some extent, should disobey. Can kids manipulate their parents? Yes. Kind of. But it takes a certain amount of skill and emotional awareness to be able to do that. Not all kids at all ages and stages have mastered the required skills to be manipulative. Sometimes they are just being kids and we are feeling some feels about that.

· 16 ·

ARE YOU YELLING OR ARE YOU JUST LOUD?

My trigger to shifting to a more intentional, responsive style of raising my kid began with yelling. I yelled myself into reality. In my experience floating around the parenting sphere of the internet, a lot of people find themselves wanting to shift their parenting style primarily because they yell so damn much. So if that's you, know first that you are not alone. You are not failing because you yell. And you can begin to change your approach to communicating with your kids, even when pissed off.

Yelling is sort of the first outlet of emotional dysregulation. You try to keep your feelings contained but eventually the overload gets the best of you and the first release for all that pent-up rage and frustration is screaming. It might be into your pillow or at the steering wheel. But it probably ends up at, toward, because of, and with your children.

If you're this deep into a book about responsive parenting, it's safe to say you've probably said to yourself at least once, "I wish I didn't yell so much." You're not alone. We all say it. Every single one of us. Remember, we are not perfect parents raising perfect children. We are very much flawed, constantly evolving human beings attempting to raise stable, healthy, well-adjusted children to adulthood.

The real question you have to ask yourself when examining your own parental communication style is "Am I yelling or am I just loud?"

My house is just loud. A loud, noisy cacophony of never-ending sounds, shouts, music blared at too-high volume, and overlapping conversation. I honestly don't actually know what to do with myself when it's quiet. Even now as I type I've got Fall Out Boy blaring at max volume.

My hearing loss from birth combined with my husband's hearing damage from a decade of diesel engines meets with children's natural lack of volume control and the noise is never-ending. I often wonder what the delivery drivers who periodically drop stuff off on my porch think of the maelstrom that is the Laithland habitat.

I've always been a loud person. My speaking volume, laughter, silliness, anger—all of it was loud. So when I first started shifting from reactive to a more responsive, intentional parenting style, of course the yelling was top of the list of things Gwenna needed to address in herself. And of course The Big Blow-up involved yelling.

It didn't take long for me to notice a distinction between yelling and being loud. And thus a line was drawn between the two. Disclaimer: Yes, ultimately, it would be wonderful if we could never raise our volume to be heard over the din. We would always be able to stop what we are doing, go to where our children are, and communicate with them at regular speaking volumes. That would be so lovely. It's also wildly unreasonable and not always feasible. No one drops everything anytime they need to say a word or two to a human located in another room. The argument could be made that perhaps we should. But we don't.

There are plenty of times when "shouting" across the house is normal.

"Dinner is ready!"
"Let the dog out!"
"Did you wipe your butt and wash your hands?"
"What's that smell?"

For the purposes of this book I'm going to draw a line in the sand. There is a difference between yelling and shouting. It should be made clear that this distinction is not universally agreed upon. The English language (the language I shout in my home) is imprecise.

Yelling is emotionally driven, charged, or motivated. It is both a release and can be used as a weapon of intimidation.

Shouting is communication with elevated volume or, occasionally, elevated urgency.

With that in mind, imagine how the same phrase would be yelled versus how it would be shouted. I'm betting the difference in your mind has a lot to do with tone. You can yell, "Put that down," and it's going to sound and feel different than simply shouting, "Put that down."

Both levels of communication are (hopefully) going to yield

the same result; whatever is up that shouldn't be is put down. But when your emotions are high, your tone is pretty rough, and the anger is seeping through your command, you're yelling. You are unregulated and at the end of your rope.

When your tone is controlled, your emotions stable (even if you're angry, you can be stable), and the only thing that is elevated is your volume, you're shouting. You're going to convey urgency but not threaten.

Most yelling is cathartic. It is the physical release for a lot of emotions and not exclusively the "bad, mad, sad" ones. Think about cheering on a sports team or losing your goddamn mind at your favorite musician's concert. You are yelling with joy, enthusiasm, enjoyment. But that level of communication is still emotionally driven.

Shouting, on the other hand, is just being louder than whatever is going on that requires you to lift your volume. If you ask my kids, they'd say I yell. Again, my distinction between yelling and shouting is not a universally accepted truth. And truth be told, yeah, sometimes I yell. Sometimes I lose my cool and my temper and yell. But more often than not, I'm shouting.

This is especially true in a vehicle. I am an anxious driver. I don't like cars. I prefer to fly, boat, or train when possible. I'm an even more anxious passenger. Something about lacking control of the vehicle I already mistrust, while surrounded by other vehicles I also mistrust being operated by other humans who I trust even less than I trust the vehicles, sends me into a tailspin of worry and cramming down panic attacks.

So it's great that my family and I moved to the middle of nowhere and I routinely have to spend anywhere from twenty minutes to an hour to get somewhere. It's also fantastic that my kids are at their noisiest when bored. You know, like one would be when strapped into a car seat for twenty minutes to an hour.

Now, since I know my triggers, I've taken steps to be able to keep myself from making my car-based anxiety my kids' problem. I listen to audiobooks and keep fidget toys in the minivan. But I also know that I'm going to shout a lot. When my kids drive up the volume to the point I can no longer focus on my audiobook, I'll lift my volume to be just above theirs and keep it there just until I have both their attention and focus. Once I'm sure they are with me and able to hear me over road noise, the car stereo, and their own raucous sound effects, I can lower my volume to match.

"HEY! MINIVAN MAFIA! YOU NEED to lower the volume a few clicks. You are making outside sounds inside a very small van. For our safety and my sanity you need to be quieter than Mom's book on the car radio."

According to my kids, this is yelling. But to me it is a communication tool wherein being louder than my kids is the only tool at my disposal. I can't stop what I'm doing and turn around and address them calmly and coolly, at their level, while doing seventy-five on the interstate. So, shouting became my only inroads to getting their attention. Once their volume falls to subsonic levels, my volume falls as well. This is a version of matching energy. I'm only as loud as I need to be to be heard and only for as long as it takes to get attention.

Neil Strauss, author and speaker, once said:

> When you yell at your children, you aren't teaching them discipline. You're teaching them how to yell. One of the biggest gifts you can give your children is your own emotional regulation.

The difference between yelling and shouting really comes down to control. Are you choosing this volume and communication style, or was it chosen for you by your mood, frustration, or emotional overload? Are you in control of your feelings, or are they in control of you?

But Gwenna, what about calmly repeating yourself and attention getters like "catch a bubble" or "quiet coyote"?

Excellent question. As always. Yes, those types of crowd-control, attention-grabbing methods of communication can absolutely be effective and I sometimes use them, depending on what is going on and how quickly I need to wrangle the situation. But in this specific instance, with the car anxiety and noisy kids and needing to maintain my own emotional control, the shouting was the quickest way to get the kids' attention before my anxiety took over and I was no longer in control of my emotions.

If you are fresh to responsive parenting, remember, it begins with you. Being able to assess your triggers, regulate (not suppress, regulate) your emotions, and communicate calmly even when pissed are going to go a long way in helping you avoid the yelling.

But so too will some grace and discernment as to whether you are yelling or just being loud. Yes, even responsive parents lose their shit. Kids can be real assholes sometimes. You will still yell. But, pop quiz from an earlier chapter: What do we do when we lose our shit and yell? YES! We apologize. Everyone is entitled not just to bad moods but poor choices on how to handle those bad moods.

Gwenna, you already covered apologies. Like really, really well. You're sort of circling the drain here.

No, this is an intentional form of communication, just like

my choice to shout *over* my kids as opposed to yelling *at* them. Apologies are incredibly important and seeing as we are flawed humans trying to help other humans not be flawed in the same way, we will give ourselves plenty of reason and opportunity to practice the art of "I'm sorry."

The difference between an emotionally aware human and one who is still ruled entirely by the ebb and flow of their feelings is the ability to recognize when we lost that shit, gather up what we can, and apologize to those it landed on. This is especially true when it comes to the relationship between a parent and a child.

FIELD GUIDE ENTRY: *Panic and Fear*

There will be times when your kids scare the ever living daylights out of you. And not just the weird goblin ninja thing they do in the middle of the night or by jumping out and scaring you. If you haven't already experienced what I'm talking about, I promise there will be at least one moment where your physical body wants to pee, vomit, poop, and pass out all at the same time. I'm talking fun little disappearing acts, darting toward traffic, near misses with dangerous acts or outcomes, mystery illnesses, and too much time on Dr. Google. Moments will come wherein you truly believe you are about to watch your child expire in front of you. Sometimes because your kid makes a fascinating choice with total disregard for their self-preservation instinct. They suck at both risk assessment and impulse control—a very dangerous combination of brain development for a human who also cannot tie their shoes or feed themselves without assistance—and sometimes because the stars or fates or situation aligned in a perfectly imperfect way and your child was simply at the wrong place at the wrong time.

Nevertheless, your child will induce fear and panic in you. In these cases, you will very likely fall into purely reactive parenting, often out of necessity. This may be screaming at them to move or pay attention. This may bring all those big mad, sad, scared feelings to the surface where they are much harder to regulate. It will stretch your emotional control so thin it almost feels as if it has snapped entirely.

In these cases, I will never advocate for just letting yourself snap. I will say if you manage to keep yourself contained and calm and not screaming in terror, I'm going to be exceedingly impressed and will have some questions for you in the aftermath as to how you fucking did that because Imma need some pointers. Occasionally, very occasionally, it can be useful to show your kid just how scared or panicked you were for their health and safety, especially if we are talking about universal dangers like playing a game of chicken with a Peterbilt or trying a "magic trick" with the pilot light on the stove.

You're probably going to yell just a bit when you discover, prevent, or save their inattentive little asses from the near-death experience they didn't realize they'd had. Yep, you're still going to have to apologize later but again, you are entitled to your own feelings. And both panic and fear are some of the hardest to keep good control over.

This is where I typically remind folks you do not have to be a gentle person to be a gentle or responsive parent. You can let them see your emotions high, your eyes wide with fear, and how much you're struggling to remember how to breathe on manual. Ultimately, you're trying not to terrorize your children into obedience. But also, some fear is reasonable and healthy. It's a natural response and safety mechanism built into our brains. Kids, with their underdeveloped brains, might not always be scared of the "right" things. Seeing their parents' reactions is important to learning that oncoming traffic is dangerous and should be handled with care.

Our job as parents is not to prevent bad things from happening to them but to give them the guidance to cope with bad things when they do happen. One of those coping methods is a healthy amount of both fear and awareness of things that could really hurt us or others. Seeing that this frightened their parent and, in turn, how their parent handled that fear is vital in them understanding how to process their own fear and panic.

TL;DR

As responsive parents we are aiming for controlled, emotionally aware communication as often as possible. Notice it says "as often as possible." Not always. There is a difference between yelling to dominate or belittle and just raising your volume over the noise of childhood. Being in control of your own emotions is often the difference between the two. Gwenna talks about apologizing to your kids for the billionth time.

· 17 ·

IT'S OKAY IF YOU HATE PLAYING CANDYLAND

It was a stormy May Saturday afternoon when I realized that I had lost a part of my childhood. For those of you not from Oklahoma or another tornado alley state, the month of May is typically the height of our storm and tornado season. Power grid failures are common as the winds, hail, and driving rain mess with overstressed power poles and down trees onto the lines. It was one such afternoon when the power flickered, wavered, and then switched off. The rain pelted the window and it was darker than it should have been for three p.m. Thunder rolled overhead as my then three-year-old daughter and I sat admiring the storms.

Being a good Oklahoma girl, I raised my daughter with a respect for storms as opposed to a fear. She enjoyed watching the lightning and listening to the thunder as much as I did. Unfortunately she was still three and had about a two-minute attention span. That's probably being generous. Moments after the lights faded away, she announced she was bored.

"Let's play the candy game," she declared. It wasn't so much a request as it was a demand. She meant Candyland. My mom had just purchased it for her and we'd yet to even open the box. My daughter had been immediately drawn to the box with all its colors and sweet, tantalizing candy-themed characters. With the power out and the storm raging I couldn't think of a reason not to. And honestly I was pretty excited to break out the board game. I'd loved playing Candyland as a young girl.

After reminding my preschooler multiple times that the game Candyland involved no actual candy, we set the board up, shuffled the color square cards, and selected our pieces. I drew a card, hip-hopped my piece to the first green square, and signaled my daughter to take her turn. And that's when it happened. Ever watch videos of glacier chunks breaking away and falling into the ocean? They are very dramatic but almost feel as if they are in slow motion. That was the sensation I felt as I watched an intrinsic part of my childhood crumble and fall away. Good fucking god, Candyland is boring as shit.

I fought the good fight playing that endless game with my daughter. It took everything in me not to pick the whole board up and chuck it out into the storm. The candles I'd lit flickered mercilessly while I used every ounce of my willpower to keep playing. It was interminable. And when my piece was a precious few cards away from landing on King Candy and ending this fresh new hell of motherhood, I drew a motherfucking Plumpy card. By the rules of the game I should have returned my piece to the sugar plum troll almost all the way at the start of the game board. I didn't. I cheated. I told my daughter we just got to ignore that card since we'd already passed it.

And you know what? I felt no shame at all. Did I lie to her? Yeah. I did. But I was a grown adult and I'd been at it for an hour. I was gassed, tapped out. I couldn't do it anymore and with the end so close I couldn't reset again and go for another hour. I hated playing Candyland.

And that's okay. Something happened to parenting culture somewhere around the turn of the millennium. Maybe it was the industrialization of household chores, maybe it was the technological revolution. Maybe it was the internet and the culture it created. Maybe it was the rise of the Mommy Bloggers. I don't know. But all of a sudden it became parents' jobs not only to educate and protect their spawn but to entertain them.

We got this notion in our heads that it was all on us, the parents, to make sure their brains developed properly. We had to monitor their stimulation, provide constant input, and guide them through activities designed to enrich and engage their developing minds. And that's not untrue. This is not a "back in the day" rant. Most parents of days gone by definitely didn't do much for their kids' enrichment. It wasn't even on their radar that a child's brain can be refined by thoughtful play.

There were some good reasons for that. Chores took a hell of a lot longer when our grandparents or great-grandparents were mere tots. Laundry, as an example, was an entire day-long affair, as precious few families had automatic washing machines. Most households were using some version of scrub boards and wringers to wash the family's clothes, with mothers dipping their hands in watery lye for hours on end. Food prep took longer as a lot of our more modern, processed, easier-to-access foods didn't exist or were harder to get a hold of. Many clothes were made in the home as opposed to bought at the store or crafted by a tailor. That took time.

It meant that there weren't copious hours of free time to play with the kids. They were left to their own devices to entertain or enrich themselves. But as washing machines became affordable, microwaves got popular, and TV dinners stopped tasting like ass, families found themselves with an unprecedented amount of free time. A lot of folks turned their attention to the well-roundedness and entertainment needs of their womb fruit. Then came the expectation that this was how you were supposed to parent.

Kid-centric activities became the bread and butter of hanging out with your spawn. While board games like Candyland and Chutes and Ladders had existed for the better part of a century by the 2000s, parents were now expected to play with their kids instead of kids playing with other kids.

And that feels just . . . silly. Those games were and are targeted to kids for a reason. They aren't supposed to be entertaining to adults and yet so many of us find ourselves personally victimized by Lord Licorice and Gramma Nut. Or maybe it's LEGOs, Barbies, or tiny plastic tea sets. Perhaps it's outings to the park, ball pits, or Chuck E. Fucking Cheese. Whatever the childish vice, parents are expected to play with their kids in every spare moment. Failing to do so is failing at parenting.

Think of it this way. Imagine you've made a new friend as an adult and this new friend is an avid hiker. They live and breathe the trails. It's all they ever want to talk about or do together. If you aren't much on hiking, chances are pretty great you aren't going to want to hang out with that human terribly often. On the flip side, if you adore cross-stitch and that's all you offer to do with them, they aren't going to elect to chill with you if cross-stitch isn't really their cup of tea.

That dynamic of interaction would not sustain a healthy relationship and you would probably drift apart. It might even get to the point that you actively avoid each other.

Now let's add another dimension to this hypothetical. If you, the cross-stitcher, and they, the hiker, both share a love of Star Wars, you are far more likely to routinely do the friend thing as Star Wars is your shared activity. If you're good at friending, you'll likely go hiking with them occasionally and they might sit and cross-stitch a to-scale Boba Fett with you.

Why does cultivating quality time with our younglings feel any different? This chapter is not advocating never playing with your kids. And if you love Candyland, wonderful. I'm not jealous but I love that for you. Chances are pretty great there's another inane game, activity, or outing that makes you want to claw your own eyes out. Here's something that should feel pretty relieving. You don't have to do the eye-clawing thing. Not often, anyway.

Yes, as parents, sometimes we squash down our own needs or desires for the good of our children. Probably more often than is healthy, if we're being honest. After realizing that I hate Candyland, I did still have to play it. My daughter was an only child at the time, I was a single mother, and we lived in a fairly child-free apartment complex. If she wanted to play Candyland, I was it. But I did try to meter how often we picked that game to play. Alternatively I introduced her to Battleship, one of my favorite board games, and she was into it. When she was older we attempted Boggle. She hates that game but will occasionally agree to play it with me.

Find activities that are shared interests and use those to balance doing the things you secretly, inwardly despise. That's going to take some trial and error and that's okay. This helps you not reach the end of your emotional rope quite so quickly and fosters an understanding of how interpersonal dynamics work for your small human.

When working with or around infants you hear the term "self-soothe" a lot. It is a baby's ability to calm themselves down and to trust their caregiver's ability to meet their needs. I propose that after we've mastered, or at least improved, the self-soothing ability, we should start addressing self-amusement. This will later turn into self-motivation.

Your child's brain will continue to develop normally if they are required to find something to entertain themselves for a bit. I'm betting you are like me and have provided them with copious numbers of toys for their amusement. It's okay if you encourage them to go play with those—without you. This might also take some trial and error, not to mention trust.

Yes, you'll have to trust your kids' game selection because they will be questionable at best from time to time. And they will still probably be out of their room with a question, complaint, request, or brag every thirty-two seconds. Again, responsive parenting does not automatically equal responsive childing. They will still crave your attention and approval, rightfully so. But the more often you can encourage and allow independent play, the more you're equipping them with the ability to self-amuse.

TL;DR

You don't have to like playing every game your child loves. That's actually kind of normal. Kid games and activities are designed for kids. There's a reason many adults grew out of those kid-oriented games. Yes, sometimes you'll have to play silly games you don't really like with your kids because time with them is valuable. But you can also share your interests with your kids. Gwenna hates the game Candyland and spent an inordinate amount of time describing that.

18

CHANCES ARE PRETTY GREAT YOUR KID JUST NEEDS TO POOP

Babies get kind of a bad rap, what with their incessant need having and infuriatingly limited communication skills. As a parent I was not a fan of the newborn stage. For the purposes of this book I define newborn stage as the first two-ish weeks of life. They sleep more than they are awake, they have awful motor skills and muscle tone, and while their cries are the most stress-inducing sound known to humankind, again, they are asleep or eating 90 percent of the time. So the crying isn't awful, all things considered.

Here's why I don't prefer that stage. (1) Newborns are freaking boring. Because of that low muscle tone as well as poor eyesight, they don't really engage. Sure, the newborn scrunch is pretty cute. (That's where when you pick them up they pull those little legs up into a fetal position.) The newborn smell is nice when you can catch it but most of the time they smell like cheese and poop. And (2) the newborn stage equips new parents, especially if it is their first baby, with this false sense of confidence. They sleep so dang much most folks fall into this trap of thinking, "You know, it's not so bad. The potato just sleeps all day and gives the best snuggles. I don't know what everyone is complaining about." Add to that, most parents have that long-lasting serotonin high from the physical act of having the child and no longer being pregnant or having a pregnant partner.

And then, the kid exits the newborn stage. There is no warning. All of a sudden your baby Rip Van Winkle can stay awake for six hours straight, screaming about something the whole time. That's when it hits most parents—the exhaustion, the confusion, the self-doubt. It all slams into you at once and there's a period of adjustment of a week to a month. Babies hit that rapid growth phase and don't give their parents time to find which way is up. It's just an avalanche of development and changing needs. About the time you figure out that the chin-hold for burping is the way to go, they stop needing that one and need the knee-lay or absolutely every ounce of fluid food is coming back up.

But ultimately, we all get the hang of it eventually. We learn to speak baby-cry. We can predict from a facial expression if they are about to go nuclear. We master the zombie-like state of functioning on impossibly small amounts of sleep. And we figure out the needs trifecta.

If baby is crying there are three things to check right away:

Is baby hungry?
Is baby tired?
Does baby need a diaper or outfit change?

It simply becomes a matter of habit to check those things first because probably half the time, the answer to "Why are you making that awful noise, youngling?" is hunger, exhaustion, or bodily fluids. If those things don't check the box and hush the pterodactyl sounds, you move on to other possible problems, but that needs trifecta is your first stop.

Note to very new or expecting parents: If you are reading this and you are either expecting, preparing for, or cuddling your newborn, hi. If you'd never heard of the needs trifecta, that's okay. First, you should know, I may have made that particular phrase up. I say "may" because there's a greater-than-none chance I read it somewhere a million years ago and just tucked that into my subconscious. Second, parenting, especially the first year, ends up relying a lot on instinct for a lot of reasons, not the least of which is because instinct is about the only brain function that continues operating through sleep deprivation. Even if parents never had a name or a handy-dandy phrase like "needs trifecta," they still end up checking those three needs first. Mostly because the needs trifecta represents the needs easiest to resolve. Our survival instinct means we are always looking for the easy way out. And if popping a boob or bottle into our screaming spawn's mouth gets the screeching to stop, we are probably going to try that first when the screeching starts back up again. Again, if this is all new information and you felt like you were just supposed to know that, no. No, you weren't. But now you do know a thing that might make having that new baby, like, 1 percent easier.

Yeah, just 1 percent. I'm trying to keep it realistic. Sorry.

But then our children play a dirty, rotten trick on us. They learn to communicate over the course of the next few years.

We learn yet another kid-centric language of toddlerese, our womb fruit learn how to pee in the potty instead of their pants, and they can outright tell us (loudly and often) that they require sustenance. We begin to listen to their demands and sometimes forget that kids really suck at knowing the difference between a want and a need.

There are times that parents find themselves mid-breakdown with absolutely no indication of what the hell is wrong. The kid was fine and then was definitely not fine. A little thing that typically does not set your tiny terrorist off has now triggered what could be the start of the apocalypse.

Yeah, chances are pretty great your kid just needs to poop. Or is hangry. Or has gotten a bit dehydrated. Or is really overtired and overstimulated. Time to check the needs trifecta. Not only will it potentially cool your little one's hellfire tantrum a bit, but it is a really good redirect.

When you are navigating a tantrum, you're playing it by ear every time. Will this thing I'm about to try make it worse? Will this technique that's worked a hundred times before backfire on me this time? The answer to both those questions is always "maybe." But you still have to try them nonetheless.

Remember, we discussed that your kid can tell you "no." So don't phrase this needs-trifecta check in a way that allows for them to deepen their tantrum and tell you "no." Of course they aren't going to *want* a drink. If it had occurred to them that they were thirsty, they would have already informed you of that. But thirsty and dehydrated can be two different sensations in both kids and adults. Rather than, "Do you want a drink?" Lead by example. Tell them, "I'm thirsty. Let's go get me a drink." Then pour yourself a small glass of water, milk, juice, whatever you'd like that your kid will drink and take a sip (or a pretend sip if you're not down with the sharing of fluids with your offspring). Then offer them a sip. Do the same with a snack. Besides prompting them to a resolution by example, it is a universal truth that anything on Mom's plate or in her cup tastes a gajillion times better than the exact same food or beverage fixed specifically for them.

Or take the fit-throwing child into the potty to do anything. Wash your hands, have a go yourself, touch up your lippie. Anything you feel comfortable and reasonable doing in the bathroom. Next to the toilet. At some point, tell them to have a go at going potty.

Doing it this way, you've done two things for tantrum mitigation. (1) You're checking the needs trifecta without dismissing the possibility that something else is triggering your kid. (2) You are changing scenery. It's going to remove them from the site wherein everything went sideways for them. It gives their little rage-soaked brains a chance to re-center and figure out where they are and why.

Okay, Gwenna. So then what happens when you check the needs trifecta and they either goblin growl nothing but those precious "nos" of yours or it doesn't seem to resolve the fit?

You're an excellent question asker. Has anyone ever told you that?

If you've checked the needs trifecta and the fit continues, you've got at least two options.

Wait it out. If you've just provided nourishment or hydration, it's going to take a bit of time for his body to communicate with itself and get said nutrients and water where they need to go. If you're laying her down for a much-needed nap, she is still going to have to burn off all those angry brain chemicals to relax enough to go to sleep. Addressing the needs trifecta isn't an immediate "stop crying" solution. But it does encompass the most common reasons kids are attempting to summon Lucifer himself.

Continue to explore. If, after giving the needs trifecta your best try this kid is still riled up, you move on to other potential issues. Overstimulation, understimulation, a communication gap, ill-fitting shoes, their sudden and without-context memory that pelicans are kinda scary. Whatever has them amped, you'll have to suss it out of a difficult-to-communicate-with miniature person who actually sort of sucks at communicating. And being a person.

Here's where you totally expect me to write down some specific steps about how to do that. And here's where it gets awkward because I am not going to do that. Not because I don't want to. I really want to. But because I can't. Once you eliminate the needs trifecta as *not* the source of their breakdown, you have to get creative again and see if you can get them to tell you what's actually wrong. (See the appendix for some co-regulation starter ideas of how to do this.) You revert back to the Big Feels Loop-De-Loo we already discussed and start from there.

Rinse and repeat.

Well, this chapter ended on a sour note. Let's go take care of ourselves, then.

TL;DR

Most acting out or misbehaving comes down to an unmet need. Or at least your kid thinks they have an unmet need. It might actually be an unmet want and you'll have to figure that out. But most of the time if your kid is being extra difficult you can tamp down that attitude by checking on the needs trifecta: Is the kid hungry/thirsty? Is the kid tired? Do they need to potty? A lot of the time helping them resolve that need makes it easier to figure out what, if anything, is actually wrong.

19

TAKING CARE OF YOURSELF IS TAKING CARE OF YOUR KIDS

Let's talk about self-care.

You know, I really debated opening this chapter with that sentence. Because personally, the minute I start reading an article or watching a video and someone says, "Let's talk about self-care," I move on. Not because I don't think self-care is important or I think it's impossible, but because probably 90 percent of those meant-to-be-helpful articles and posts fixate on this body care as self-care and that doesn't work for me. Taking care of your body (i.e., spa days, massages, nice lotions, workouts, baths, or other things that focus on the care and maintenance of your meat-sack) is only one part of self-care.

We are still going to talk about self-care, but I'm not going to spend the next several pages using flowery language to basically say, "It rubs the lotion on its skin."

First, let's define self-care. Self-care is one part of stress reduction. It is anything that makes you feel rested, recharged, or ready to face the rest of your day, your work, your tasks, or whatever you've got going on.

Gee, thanks, Gwenna, that's a nice, trite answer that can pretty much describe anything.

Yep. Exactly. That's the point.

There seems to be a dichotomy of opinions when it comes to self-care. One camp will say any time you spend focusing on yourself counts as self-care. So hop in the shower, use the good-smelling fancy soap you used to reserve for humble tumble time, and you've practiced self-care. The other side maintains that basic hygiene and fancy soap are not the same as caring for yourself, your mental state, and your meat vessel.

Personally, I'm somewhere in the middle. A shower isn't always self-care. But it can be. I have two shower modes. I have functional showers. Soap in the smelly places, a squirt of shampoo, a vigorous washing of the face, and done. I have spa showers. Water temps rivaling the core of the sun, some version of fancy mud rubbed over whatever amount of me it will cover, hair mask, getting the cheese grater thing out and going after my dragon-skin heels with it, and then just standing in the water until the hot water heater taps out. It might not sound great to you but I love my spa showers. (It should be stated here I'm not a bath girl. No shade if you love a nice soak but I don't want to stew in my own juices nor fight my ADHD to just be still. That's more work than is worth it to me.)

At any point, either of those showers can be self-care. Yes, even the quick in-and-out shower is sometimes enough to give me some pause, let me scrub off the ick, and get rid of that weird greasy-hair feeling I personally hate. That makes me feel just a tiny bit recharged. The flip side is sometimes the spa showers aren't really self-care. I come out just as exhausted but now slightly softer, lobster-colored, and smelling like a botanical garden was sacrificed in my name. I'm still ready for bed and nowhere near ready to deal with momming or adulting or wife-ing or existing.

My point here is: Any activity can be self-care. But they may not *always* be self-care. The trick is knowing when an activity is and isn't self-care.

Before we move on, let's tackle the idea that self-care can only be performed in solitude or at least in the absence of your children. Because let's be honest, if self-care is partly stress reduction, your kids are probably one of your biggest stressors. How are you supposed to reduce stress with the stressors actively trying to stress you out? In an ideal situation, yes, you can get both physical and mental distance from kids, family, housework, career, whatever. But that is not the only way to take care of yourself.

One of the things I promised myself when my two youngest children were infants was that I would get dressed every day. With infants, two at once in my case, the nights and days don't feel much different. Sleep is fleeting and you spend so much time holed up in your house, it doesn't much matter how light or dark the sky is. But I needed to mark the end of one day and the beginning of another. It was important for my mental state to make this delineation. So even if I had been awake for hours, when my husband would get up to go to work, I would get dressed. It might look like swapping one set of pajama-like athleisure wear for another just like it (leggings and T-shirts 4 LYFE!). But it was still an indicator for both body and brain that a new day had begun. That was self-care at its very core. I wasn't less tired but I did feel more ready to handle all that tiredness. Half the time I got dressed with a full audience of wide-eyed infants.

Was it the best thing I could do to take care of myself? Was it meeting every need I had? No. Absolutely not. But that's where the self-care narrative goes a little sideways. Plenty of "practice self-care" slogans are bandied about the internet but not a lot in the way of "Here's how you determine what part of you needs taking care of!" Not everything you do to take care of yourself has to be full send. Sometimes little things can go a long way to making you feel rested, recharged, or ready to face down your stressors again.

I got incredibly lucky that my kids, all three of them, generally liked being in the car. We never had the car-seat planking issue, no car sickness. Unless there were other mitigating factors (like being hangry—angry because hungry—or plum worn out) I never had to fight to get my kids in the car. Thus one of my key elements of my self-care became car rides and audiobooks. The kids would get snacks and tablets with headphones. The eldest had the whole third row to herself and I'd ply her with overpriced coffee and chicken nuggets. I would also get myself an overpriced coffee and chicken nuggets. And then we'd drive around while I listened to an audiobook. The kids were strapped in, amused, getting plenty of stimulation. They couldn't touch each other and had very little reason to interact. I got precious silence save the audiobook of my choosing and no one touching me. I looked forward to "driving time" the entire year of 2019. It was my lifeline to feeling sane.

I wasn't by myself and I actually had to do just a bit of prep work to make it happen, but those drives were integral in my self care in 2019 and the earliest parts of 2020. Other possible forms of self-care when you can't ditch the kids include:

Blippi **Breaks:** You know that one show that no matter how hard you try to tune it out, you still hear it in the background and it drives you absolutely bonkers? Your kids love it but if ever you meet any of its creators, jail may actually be a viable outcome you're willing to accept? Yeah, for just one day, ban it. I pick on *Blippi* here but it could be any show that grates your nerves in that special way. Sure, it might be useful to distract the kids, but it also pushes you deeper and deeper into burnout territory. Let your womb fruit watch anything else but for one day, send Blippi or Peppa or Barney or Twilight Sparkle on a break.

Muffin Tin Dinner: Grab a muffin tin from wherever it lives and fill each little cup with a different food. Whatever food fits. Goldfish, butter crackers, pepperoni, a fruit cup, a pile of lunch meat, a schmear of peanut butter, croutons, fruit, the dregs of whatever cereal you've got; whatever. Boom. Dinner. Low effort. Fascinating for the littles. It's like baby charcuterie. Anytime you can save yourself hassle and effort, it's going to reduce your stress, even if just by a fraction of a fraction. And since self-care is a part of stress reduction, Muffin Tin Dinner can be stress reduction.

Put On Your Pearls: Put something on that makes you feel pretty, confident, strong, or bold, even if that thing is wildly out of place for the rest of your outfit or your day. For me, it's a strand of pearls. For you it could be a deeply plunging neckline shirt or that pair of Louboutins from back before you had kids. Wear those chandelier earrings while you load the dishes. Rock those pumps at the grocery store. Swipe on that lizard-green, super glittery eyeshadow even if the rest of your face is bare. If it makes you feel a thing, it is a form of self-care. It doesn't even have to be glam. It could be wearing some fancy, lacy undergarments beneath your fuzzy pajama pants and hoodie. But anything that you put on just because you enjoy it counts. Because you can. Because you deserve to feel pretty and don't have to reserve those things for "special occasions" that seem to be getting further and further apart.

Alright, I'm gonna assume you get it. Self-care does not have to be the same thing every time. It does not have to be done in isolation or in the absence of your chaos goblins. Now here's where I have to backpedal just a bit. The best self-care is the fully immersive, escapist type of activity. Reading a book with zero chance of being interrupted, going through a day without having to make a choice on someone else's behalf, not having to wipe anyone else's butthole, and being able to disengage from your real life entirely—that's inarguably self-care. We want that. We need that. But, being honest, we can't always or often get that.

Hence we are consistently and constantly running this knife's edge of parental burnout. So we have to pick and choose these little mini self-care moments to sort of stave off the emotional exhaustion and physical fallout. But how do you know what action is going to result in the highest chance of recharge, rest, or readiness to function?

Here's the rubric I use to figure out which of my needs I should attend to first when I'm feeling that cranky, burnt-out, about-to-snap-over-little-shit cloud darkening my sky.

1. Do you need to eat or hydrate, have you had a normal poop in a while, or do you need a nap? Yep, that's the needs trifecta we talked about earlier and you are still subject to that.

    Possible self-care solutions: I default to getting some water and grabbing some grapes when I feel the fringes of a bad mood coming on. I added probiotics to my daily handful of "please don't die of weird shit you're too young for" candies (you call them vitamins). As for the naps, well, sometimes they happen, sometimes they don't. But occasionally just identifying that I need sleep can help reframe that "I'm an awful person who is fucking everything up" feeling. I'm not. I'm just tired.

2. Am I overstimulated or under-stimulated? Boredom and being touched out feel very similar to me. No body position is comfortable, no form of entertainment is actually entertaining, or I've fully dissociated from planet Earth.

    Possible self-care solutions: Change your scenery. Move yourself and/or your kids to a new place in the house. Take a drive if that's possible. Just go stand outside and get some vitamin D. Literally touch grass. Decide that maybe it's time for an impromptu movie day and table snacks. Anything that breaks the monotony of the day in/day out grind of parenting, especially if you have littles who do not yet go to school or it is summertime and everyone is just there, in the house, seeking stimulation.

3. Have I de-prioritized myself too many times in a row? As parents we often set aside our own needs in order to address the needs of our family. But that comes at a cost of pushing us closer and closer to parental burnout.

    Possible self-care solutions: Order a pizza or pour some cereal for dinner. Survival mode is possible on occasion. It is hopefully not your full-time status, but sometimes you really do have to say, "Fuck it—this is all the effort I've got left."

4. Have I checked in with my body and mind beyond the needs trifecta? A sore shoulder, unaddressed bloating, menstrual cycles, seasonal depression, regular old depression—all of these can affect your ability to function, much less parent.

    Possible self-care solutions: Go ahead and call the doctor about that one thing. If you're American and reading this, I know that isn't as straightforward as it ought to be, so do what you can with the resources you've got. If you're in pain, a part of your brain is always going to be focused on that. If you are lucky enough to *not* be living with chronic illness, part of your self-care can be addressing the source of that pain. It isn't selfish to care for yourself. Taking care of yourself is taking care of your kids.

Okay, I'm done with the numbered listicle but I'm not quite done with that last sentence I wrote there. I'm proud of that one and we're going to keep talking about it.

Taking care of yourself is taking care of your kids. Every time I've said this somewhere on the internet, I'm always met with at least one or two responses like:

"I can't afford to take care of myself AND my kids."

or

"I am all there is. I have no support. No one can watch my kids while I check out."

or

"By the time I get everyone else to the point I can take care of myself, I'm out of spoons [energy] to do anything for me."

Yeah. I get that. I've been there. In those exact places; an isolated new mother cut off from family and friends, and later a single mom working two jobs and still on food stamps, and finally a stay-at-home mom, outnumbered by her spawn and operating in states of pure exhaustion.

Ultimately though, you're allowed to simply communicate with your kid, "Mommy is tired. Mommy needs a minute." And if your first inclination is to recoil from that, let me explain why this is peak-level parenting.

Our job as parents is to parent ourselves out of a job; we want our kids to be equipped with the tools and maturity to advocate for themselves. If their manager is a slice of dick cheese and asking them to go far beyond their pay grade or compensation, we'd have no trouble advising our kid to act their age and tell them "no." If our adult child finds a partner that is just awful to them, we would wholly support "Know your worth and dump their ass." But how do we teach them to value themselves and stand up for their own needs?

You see where I'm going with this? Yeah, you do. And I can feel you still trying to argue with me that there isn't room for any of this nonsense. Okay, I hear you. I hear the fear and frustration and burnout. So I ask again, how do we teach our children to value themselves and stand up for their own needs?

We model that behavior. We value ourselves as humans who are more than "just" moms. We communicate that we need to put our own needs first. And yes, having just one goddamn moment of peace and quiet where no one is touching, needing, speaking to, or perceiving us is actually a need from time to time.

When you tell your kid that you are tired or that you need to have some alone time, even if it's just for ten minutes, you are showing them how to advocate for themselves. You are teaching by example that it is not just okay but necessary to care for your physical and mental health, even if that means putting someone else's wants aside. You demonstrate how *not* to be a people pleaser.

In the same way apologies teach our kids what to do when we make mistakes, practicing self-care teaches our kids that they can and should care for themselves. It also teaches them empathy. In order for you to take a minute, your kid first needs to know that you need a minute, and second have the empathy to grant you that moment of self-care.

So yes, taking care of yourself is taking care of your kids. It is the highest level of parenting. Take that, Arguer McArgueface.

(And that's how a professional writer ends a chapter.)

TL;DR

Self-care is anything that helps you feel rested, recharged, or more ready to handle the rest of your responsibilities. Yeah, that's it. That's the whole chapter summary. There are some ideas on how to do that too. But this whole chapter was pretty much Gwenna taking a really long time to say that self-care is anything that helps you feel rested, recharged, or more ready to handle the rest of your responsibilities. Gwenna likes alliteration.

20

LEARNING TO PERSON FROM SCRATCH

As I write this book, my youngest two children have started preschool. While for many parents, this particular milestone might bring a mixed bag of emotions, for me it was mostly celebratory. I was overjoyed to make it through infancy and toddlerhood. They are school-agers, little ones, but school-agers nonetheless. They are developing certain levels of independence. I don't have to dress them anymore. They can do that all by themselves. And if I try to help in the interest of saving a little time, I am quite clearly told they can do it "all by myself." I'm elated that we made it this far.

My one and only complaint is school drop-off line. It is a chaotic disaster of impatience and cuteness. Parents who have certainly been driving for at least a few years suddenly forget the laws of traffic. There's always that one mom who has to give eighteen butterfly kisses, tummy-tum snuggles, and recite a short limerick to her child before she lets him out of the car and gets out of the unload spot. My personal favorite is the grandpa or aunt who has never done drop-off and clogs up the whole otherwise streamlined process. I'd like to be the bigger person and not get viscerally mad at them in the moment. But I am not. The logical part of my brain can rationalize that of course it's confusing and you aren't sure where to go and everyone has to have a first time doing something but also *fucking move. Use your eyeballs and all that big brain meat to observe what literally every other car is doing!*

Apologies. There might have been an incident immediately before sitting down to write this chapter. I digress. The whole point of opening with the "my kids are in preschool and I hate drop-off line" anecdote follows.

One random Tuesday in August, my high schooler came with me to drop the littles off at preschool. The eldest typically walks to class but needed a ride because she had a rather large box to bring to school. Since the littles' school starts nearly an hour before the high school, the eldest was in the car for drop-off. As the boy- and girl-child exited the car and began walking up to the school building, my eldest observed, "They must feel so big!"

"Why do you say that?" I returned.

"Because they are walking into the school by themselves. At least it feels that way. I remember feeling like such a big kid when no teacher held my hand to walk me into the building," she replied, craning her neck to watch her siblings disappear into the door of the school.

And that gave me a moment of pause. I hadn't really thought about how important it would make them feel to walk the twelve whole feet from the car door to the school building by themselves. To a four-year-old, that distance may as well have been miles of wilderness, fraught with danger, that they were big and brave enough to conquer on the daily. In their minds they had choices. They could run to the playground or take off into the neighborhood. While in our home it wasn't their first taste of autonomy, it could very well be the most impactful taste.

Autonomy is a weird concept to teach. The dictionary definition is "the right or condition of self-government." In practice, autonomy is the ability to make decisions for oneself. On one hand, as adults we have nearly full autonomy to decide what to do with our time, bodies, effort, and mental energy. As members of a functioning society we can't go full anarchist and just start offing pigeons for fun, but we more or less have the ability to decide what, where, how, when, and why to do a thing.

Kids don't really have that. The adults responsible for them, be they parents, guardians, care providers, or teachers, tell them when to be awake, when to be clothed and often what kind of clothes to wear, when to eat, when not to eat, what to eat, what not to eat, when to focus, when to play, where to go, when to leave. Honestly for good reason. Kids have terrible impulse control and an awful sense of need versus want. We're only better at autonomy because we've had more practice. Kids are learning to person from scratch.

For the responsive parent, that means allowing autonomy as often as possible. Way back in the book, chapters and chapters ago, we talked about allowing our kids to say "no" to us and being kind of choosy about how we present questions. If "no" is not an answer we can accept, because again, kids really and truly suck at assessing actual needs, we don't phrase the question in a way they can decline.

But we can offer them the experience of autonomy in other ways. Take coming inside or leaving the park as an example. I can't offer "Do you want to go inside?" as an option because it's time to come inside. I can't accept "no" as an answer. Coming inside is the boundary I have to set. I can give them other ways to participate in the decision-making process. We want them to have some practice autonomy in a low-stakes moment. Would you like to leave the water table up for tomorrow or drain it? When we get inside would you like to have a snack first or go take your shoes off first?

We can also prevent autonomy overload. As an adult, I know I struggle with decision fatigue and overwhelm. Put me in front of a display of potato chips, have people standing there waiting for me to make a decision, and I will default to the same two or three I know I like. I'm perfectly willing to try new flavors but when the pressure is on, too many choices become overwhelming for the most stable and mature adults. It's doubly overwhelming for pre-adult life forms.

When my oldest was just learning to get dressed by herself, I found myself engaged in a seemingly endless battle of the bedroom. I knew I wanted to let her make her own choices. I also knew I'd intentionally purchased a mix-and-match wardrobe. Pretty much every shirt would look acceptable with any pair of pants. Endless combinations, fewer tutu-with-the-Christmas-sweater-in-June experiences. Nevertheless it is a constant process of begging and cajoling and reminding and encouraging.

Please put your pants on.

And your socks.

Yes, both socks.

Okay, and now shoes. Sure.

You're not wearing a shirt, but cool.

Why are you taking your socks off now?

Put your shoes on.

Okay, pick a shirt.

Literally any shirt.

That one is perfect. Head in hole.

Yes, I love that shirt.

Why are you putting it back?

No, you only need one shirt.

You pick or I pick, those are your options here.

Most mornings this process would culminate in my losing my shit because that shit is really, really frustrating and easy to lose. My mom suggested something to me in the midst of one of my many, many rants on motherhood on the phone. She said, "What if instead of all the clothes, she had two outfits to choose from?"

That was a lightbulb moment. The width and breadth of her entire wardrobe at her disposal was overwhelming. Too many choices, too much thought behind each piece. I'd gone just a touch further than she was ready to go with the autonomy. I needed to give her space to make her own decisions but she needed more guidance than I'd been giving. The following morning I distilled her autonomy to two outfits. Surprising outcome here, she didn't wear either of them. But she did immediately know which outfit she did want to wear. She was dressed in under ten minutes, a feat I didn't know was possible at the time.

We would continue this "Mom picks two outfits, she immediately knows what to wear and it's neither of the outfits

Mom picked" for another couple of years before she had the confidence and executive function to choose outfits without my involvement.

Autonomy is learned in small increments. That's what I learned with the wardrobe experiment. If you went to college or experienced an early adulthood prior to having kids or making a family, chances are pretty great you felt the tremendous crush of having all the choices to make. Do I pay rent or buy the gaming system? Do I buy the super responsible tuna and ramen pack or do I get sushi and have no food for the week? At least that was my experience when I got to college. All the autonomy left plenty of room for bad decision-making.

As parents our goal is to parent ourselves out of a job. (I know, I keep repeating that. It's important and you're almost finished reading the book. I'm honestly running out of pages to really drive this point home.) This means letting our children try on autonomy in little, controlled increments.

It also means being willing to let them fail safely. My eldest was finishing up her seventh-grade year when the school sent home the schedule selection paper for her eighth-grade year. It was the first year she was going to be able to select a few of her classes. All previous years her only available electives had been given to her athletics because of how our school district handles physical education and sports.

She was absolutely ecstatic to be able to choose her classes and I intentionally put no boundaries on her. Her core classes were required by the school so it didn't really matter to me what additional classes she pursued. She desperately wanted to be in a particular art class. I told her to fill out the form and turn it in early as this class was always popular and filled up quickly. And then I backed away and watched. I watched that form sit on the table for one week, and then two. I reminded her to turn in her enrollment form. And it sat for another week.

I'll give you one guess as to what happened. Yeah, she didn't get in the class. It was full by the time she turned in her enrollment form. She asked me if I could call the school. I said no. Not only could I not call the school as I had no power to change this, but even if it were in my power, I wouldn't. She had the opportunity and the autonomy to make the decisions required to get her in the class and did not. And not for a lack of support. I did remind her. Several times. What I did not do was force her hand. I let her fail. Safely.

She did not take the art class. She did get *an* art class but not the one she wanted. And she was low-key mad at me for weeks when eighth grade started. Really she was mad at herself, but I was an easy target. We talked about it once she settled into her class.

It is the worst feeling watching your kid fail at something you know full well you could have intervened in. I could have been way more proactive with that enrollment form. But this particular mistake felt pretty low-stakes in the grand scheme of things. I'd rather her learn the lessons of time management and executive function early in her life. It's going to be much easier to deal with the fallout of the failure when her parents are right there with a shoulder to cry on and some help regulating and accepting the consequences.

The more opportunities we give our children to make decisions, to fail safely, to experiment with what it means to make a choice and how those choices impact not just them but others around them, the more we are preparing them for doing the same when they've moved half a country away.

Here's a quick flow chart on how to offer your kids autonomy and the chance to fail safely.

You'll notice if you read the flow chart all the way. And be honest, you almost didn't. That's okay. I don't read graphics correctly until called out either. But now that you have read the flow chart all the way, the last question you have to ask yourself is, are you in a place to deal with the risk of failure?

When raising children, we have to do and put up with a lot. And we don't have it in us to do it all the time. That's okay.

THE DECISION-MAKING DECISION MAKER

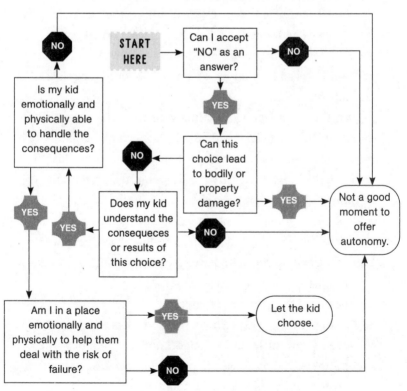

Sometimes we have to forgo a teachable moment or two because we are tapped, gassed, spent, empty—whatever metaphorical term does it for you. You can intervene and save yourself the fallout from time to time. It shouldn't be the default to just fix it for them and avoid the consequences of your kids' decision-making. But sometimes, if you can honestly say you don't have it in you and it isn't coming from a place of not wanting to see your kid reach that failure point, you can say, "Not today, kid."

TL;DR

A key element in responsive parenting is not just granting autonomy to kids but teaching them what to do with it. Kids spend most of their earliest years with grown-ups calling the shots. But at some point they need to be both allowed and taught how to make good decisions for themselves. Start small with more inconsequential decisions, like red socks or blue socks. Build from there. Allowing your kids to fail safely is also a way to teach autonomy. Gwenna made a flow chart.

21

PEANUT BUTTER AND JELLY

My husband, Jackson, and I are a dichotomy of relationship clichés. We often joke that we are the same person in different packages, that we have the same brain, or that together we are one functioning adult.

Alternatively, we have wildly different opinions on a wide range of ideologies and topics. He is a little more conservative politically, I'm a little more liberal. We are not so far apart we can't find middle ground, but in certain debate spaces we find ourselves on opposite sides of the fence. We are the couple that goes to a restaurant, orders two dishes, and dissects them of the parts one likes but the other doesn't. Salad tomatoes to him, and I'll take your olives, thank you. Here's your big ol' slab of red onion from my pasta, and I'll take those mushrooms right there.

One area we fundamentally disagree in is the proper construction of a peanut butter and jelly sandwich. My way, or rather the correct way, is to take two big fluffy slices of white bread and spread the jam or jelly of your choice on one slice but not quite to the edge. That little sliver of naked bread on the jelly slice is vital.

On the second slice you spread the peanut butter of your choice. Go as thick or thin as you prefer. I'll not shame you for your brand. I don't care if you want smooth or crunchy. I do care that you take that peanut butter schmear all the way to the edge of that slice. This way, when you press those two cloud-like slices together, that peanut butter seals in your jelly. No jelly squirts.

Did I overthink the process of constructing a simple sandwich? Maybe. But it's a comfort food for me. Some of the brightest memories of my childhood include a PB&J on Sunbeam white bread.

And then I met Jackson and his heathen ways. He mixes it. He puts the peanut butter down and then unceremoniously dumps a wad of jelly right in the center. But his real crime happens after that. He uses the knife and swirls it all together into this nightmarish paste of unevenly distributed flavors and textures. Slapping another slice on top of it, he eats it. Mixed and pasty. He even has the audacity to like it that way. It's indecent.

Gwenna, it can't possibly make a difference. You're just gonna shove it in your face, mash it up with your head bones, and swallow it. It's going to mix in your mouth. You're being dramatic.

Yes, I know, but goddammit, there's a difference. I want my tongue to dance in an unhomogenized cacophony of textures and flavors for just a moment. I want my mouth to feel the coolness of the fruit spread, the gooey peanut butter, the soft springiness of the bread before I masticate it to an ooze and cram it down my gullet. Jackson blasphemes with the skipping-the-mouthfeel part.

Should we ever divorce, his hellish way of making a peanut butter and jelly sandwich will be cited in our grounds for separation.

Wow, Gwenna. You have strong feelings about peanut butter and jelly. Why is this in a parenting book?

It's in this book because it turns out that our disagreement on how to make a peanut butter and jelly is the perfect analogy for partnered or co-parenting approaches.

I may heartily protest Jackson's ludicrous mixing method. He may find my peanut-butter-seal method too finicky. But when all is said and done, we still both end up with a peanut butter and jelly sandwich. We could each make a sandwich in our own way, show it to a total stranger, and they'd be able to identify it as a peanut butter and jelly sandwich.

The same goes for parenting. We don't have to have identical techniques at every turn so long as our goals are aligned. Ultimately, our aim is to help our spawn grow and develop into happy, healthy, stable individuals who can exist without us. How we get there can be different and will change as we all grow together as parents and as children.

There's more than one way to get to Disneyworld. If I fly and Jackson drives, as long as we know when we're supposed to be there and plan accordingly, neither of us is wrong and our destination isn't going to move. (Probably. Florida is a weird place. Shout-out to my Floridian readers.)

Both my husband and I are responsive parents in that we

keep our womb fruits' emotional development on equal standing with their functional development. But our orders of operation are a little different.

I'm more of an "ask, explain, complete." Jackson is more of an "ask, complete, explain." Both of us give space for processing feelings and figuring out how to cope with and function in the big and small emotions. Both versions of responsive parenting are effective. Neither is more right or "better." It allows both Jackson and me to be mindful of our own emotional states. I am, far and away, more emotive and volatile than my husband. That's not to say he is emotionless or that I fly off the handle at every little stimulus. But my swing from emotion to emotion is much quicker and the pendulum swings further into the "big feelings" zone. However, I'm very aware of where I am, what I'm feeling, and why. Jackson is steadier than I am, but it takes him just a little longer to process and recognize where he is.

Given that we spend some time introspecting about how and why we feel and what it takes to shift our emotional states, our distinct yet similar parenting styles work for us. We don't have to have the same approach for our kids to have a safe, protective environment to begin parsing out their own feels.

So how do you begin to parse out who parents how?

You chat. A lot. And often. And if you're just beginning to explore responsive parenting as an option for how to raise a happy, healthy human who can exist without you, you're gonna have to talk to your spouse/partner/co-parent about what that looks like.

Neat, Gwenna. How does that "chat" even start?

Excellent question. And as with all things there is no one-size-fits-all solution. But never fear, I am prepared. Here are some talking points you might address when deciding if responsive parenting is something you want to tackle in your home.

What type of human do we hope our kids will be?

- What is the most important thing for our kids to learn/know/understand in order to thrive in the adult world?
- What is something we felt we learned too late?
- What is one thing we didn't get as kids that we very much want to make sure our kid gets?
- What is one thing we did get or experience as kids that we want to make sure our kid doesn't?
- If our kid learns one and only one thing from us as humans, what do we hope that one thing is?

Those are just baseline talking points. Parenting is hard no matter how you approach it. But this handful of questions and the discussion they will hopefully spawn are a part of being intentional about how you are raising your kids.

Sidebar: For those of you in the throes of single parenting, these are still really valid questions to consider. You might not have a partner to share these ideas or thought processes with but they are still really important things to give space to.

FIELD GUIDE ENTRY:
Responsive Parenting When Your Co-Parent Doesn't "Co" Well

I never, ever get to speak on true co-parenting work. The only information I can share is that which I've learned mostly through my own experience and any research those experiences spawned. I've never successfully co-parented.

It should be stated here that I'm using co-parenting specifically for couples/family units that have, for whatever reason, split or divorced. Since there's a child in the mix a couple must still interact for the sake of the kid. Many families are able to strike a good balance of setting aside their personal feelings and history and focusing on the well-being of the tiny human who didn't ask to be born to parents who weren't great as a couple.

I am divorced. But I never co-parented. Not for my lack of trying. No, I'm not bad-mouthing my ex. But upon our divorce, I spotted and began addressing my own issues of identity, security, self-worth, and self-image. He . . . did not do those things. He blamed me for giving up and taking his daughter. We both needed therapy. Only one of us was able to accept and pursue that.

As a result, we constantly encountered issues trying to raise the child we created together. These issues looked a lot like I'd speak, he'd ignore. The dissolution of our marriage was complicated and two-sided. I recognized that even before the ink was dry on our divorce decree. But his own demons got in the way of his ability to be the father his daughter needed.

There was a lot of wheel spinning in the early days of the custody and visitation arrangement. I desperately tried to get him to at least be in the same book much less in the same chapter or page with me. Never worked. Find wall; bang head here.

So what do you do when your kid spends up to half their

time in a home where responsive parenting isn't a practice? You double down on what you do at home. Sometimes that feels like doing nothing.

We won't always be there to co-regulate with them, name their big feel, handhold while they sort out their emotions, and provide space to do those things. In an ideal world everyone would be mindful and give space for emotional understanding and processing. The truth is that the majority of humans your child will interact with don't, won't, or can't care about how anyone feels. Unfortunately that can include your child's other parent.

FIELD GUIDE ENTRY:
Teachers, Conscious Discipline, and the Rest of the World

When I was in middle school I had what might well have been the worst teacher on the planet. They taught algebra and on the very first day of class they stood up, told us their name, and promptly informed us that this would be the hardest class we'd ever taken up to that point in our academic careers. This teacher reasoned that if at least five of us twenty-ish didn't fail this class they weren't doing their job to push us mentally. The teacher also informed us that their very presence in our classroom was a great blessing to us as they were also an adjunct professor at our local community college and they could be teaching grown adults advanced math. Oh how lucky we were they were deigning to educate eighth graders because they felt it was important to shape the future generations and instruct us properly.

We were then handed the test that would ultimately be our Algebra 1 final exam and told to complete it. We did. At least we tried. We all failed miserably as we had not yet learned any of it.

That was the first grade we received in the class. A big, fat, ugly F. We started the class failing and had to work up from there.

This teacher would routinely remind us that we were all failing their class and that we needed to work harder to fix that grade. That *they* gave us. The fact that we didn't know as much as a trained and practiced adult was weaponized against middle schoolers. We spent that whole semester being belittled for not knowing as much as the teacher paid to teach it to us. I vividly remember one specific incident wherein a classmate had the audacity to ask a question about quadratic equations. The teacher turned around from the whiteboard, put their hands on their hips, and screamed, "Are you dumb? I already told you that. If it didn't sink into your thick skull, I can't help you."

None of us asked any more questions. We all struggled silently. It's no surprise that I still have a hate/hate relationship with math. That class should have been the first time I was challenged by a concept. As a gifted and talented kid (translated here as undiagnosed ADHD kid) most things came viciously easy. Including math. And then Algebra 1 ruined it all. Well, the teacher did. They taught me to fear math, to dread it, and to avoid it at all costs. Those lessons stuck. I don't remember how to do quadratic equations. I can never solve for x. And y can fuck all the way off.

They were genuinely a bad teacher and that's not a label I apply lightly. Teaching is hard. And done by humans who get to make mistakes and bad judgment calls and have to wrangle classrooms full of tiny humans from all different backgrounds and parentages. A teacher struggling with the balancing act that is public education is not a bad teacher. It's a teacher that needs better support in most cases. But that teacher, my Algebra 1 teacher, they were just bad at their job.

As a responsive parent, it is concerning when your mini me is in a class with a teacher who may not only suck at teaching, but seems to go out of their way to invalidate your kiddo's feelings and who they are as a person. What are you supposed to do about that?

Unpopular opinion time: not much. Put yourself in recovery mode for when that teacher really does a number. Now, this does not mean ignore it. You can talk to the school administrators if the teacher is really doing injurious or harmful things to your beta-version human. But if they are technically doing their jobs but just being shitty about the interpersonal stuff, well, that's one more icky-feeling lesson a responsive parent gets to tackle. Not all people will give a damn about your feelings. The pessimists would go so far as to say most people won't.

At least if your kids are encountering a person who is dismissive and emotionally unaware, they are doing so while still living at home with you, their parent who is trying their best to be the opposite of that. You get that chance you didn't want: to discuss what happens when other people don't care about your feelings or worse, actively try to give you bad ones.

Again, and not for the last time (sorry, not sorry), parents are consistently and constantly working to parent themselves out of a job. That means preparing them for people who don't care.

TL;DR

When it comes to how you parent your children with a spouse, partner, or co-parent, you don't necessarily have to be on the same page, just in the same book. Your child will encounter humans who don't give a damn about their feelings and there isn't much you can do to prevent that. You can, however, equip them with the tools they need to handle those emotionally unaware or intentionally hurtful people. Gwenna went into extraordinary detail describing peanut butter and jelly sandwiches.

22

RESPONSIVE PARENTING FOR NON-PARENTS

A dmittedly it seems like a weird move to include a chapter specifically for non-parents in a parenting book. I see that. Gonna do it anyway, and it's the last chapter of the book. You've made it this far. Might as well wrap it up.

When I say this chapter is for non-parents, that doesn't mean it can't apply to parents.

As you've read through this book, you've no doubt thought of a couple of grown-ass humans you might try some of this on. We've likely all had that one boss who was about as emotionally mature as a plank of wood. We've encountered Karens in the wild, either as a spectator or the victim of her wrath as a service industry or food service worker. We've had that one family member, teammate, or dude-bro at the gym who really can't seem to feel their feelings in a healthy way. They really do make it everyone else's problem.

So while reading through this book, it might seem like

some of these methods of negotiation with emotional neo-phytes could apply to humans who aren't your kids. Or children at all. And you're absolutely not wrong.

Before we continue, it is my strong conviction that you cannot responsively parent a human being who is not your birth, procured, or inherited child. Not because you cannot be responsive to other people, but because you can't parent people who aren't your kids.

Ultimately any version of responsive, intuitive, intentional, respectful, or gentle parenting is less about raising good kids and more about raising good humans. That means that all these techniques of identifying emotions, responding with empathy and patience, regulating and working with the feelings instead of cramming them aside to build up bitterness, resentment, or explosivity later are not skills exclusive to use in childhood and on children.

The expectation is there that we are, in fact, helping shape humans who remain emotionally aware into adulthood and have learned self-regulation even when their nerves are frayed and their mental energy drained. They are capable of expressing and maintaining autonomy as well as setting, communicating, and holding boundaries.

So yes, these ideas absolutely translate to how you cope with your own feelings and how you communicate with and through emotion to others in your life. You can absolutely use the Big Feels Loop-De-Loo when dealing with that one chick who passive-aggressively cc's your manager at the slightest hint you're about to disagree with whatever she just emailed. You can verbalize your emotions and explain the feelings you're having as you are setting or enforcing or reenforcing or re-explaining or re-re-re-enforcing a boundary with your mouthy father-in-law.

There are some slight shifts I'd recommend if applying these emotional awareness techniques on your peers, co-workers, friends, and family. Most of what you'll be doing is regulating yourself and enforcing the boundaries you need to do so.

It is still important to label the feeling. This is not only going to help you process what's happening in your brain but begin to cue other folks to check their own emotional state. Leave out a lot of the questions. Don't ask how they are feeling and don't ask permission to feel your own feels.

"Becky, I'm getting pretty frustrated by the redundant communication here."

If the emotion is shared, you can go ahead and use that intuition and name it for you both.

"Kevin, I'm just as annoyed as you are."

Next, straight-up say what you need in response to this feeling. This is that boundary setting in real-world application.

"I'm going to walk away from this cubical and take five minutes to reset and hydrate. I'll be back in one hot second."

You can add the natural consequence in as well.

"If we continue this discussion, I'm going to lose my ability to communicate well. Let's change the subject or take a break for a bit and we can resume this tomorrow/in an hour/once you get your brain out of your ass." (Maybe not that last time frame. Probably not that last time frame.)

And then (and this is the hard part), enforce that boundary. Walk the eff away. Take the five minutes. Change the topic. Cram some turkey in your mouth so you look like a squirrel and can't say what you really want to say because your head hole is full of poultry. You know it will make the situation and your emotional state worse to continue to engage. You set the boundary. Now hold it. Finally, know your regulation techniques. Not every regulation will work in every situation. You might need a walk. You might need a water. You might need to just unclench your jaw and breathe. But you know what you're feeling, you've set the boundary you need to respond to that feeling, now regulate yourself. See the co-regulation index at the back of this book for more ideas. Yes, those are geared for kids, but I promise if you go around shouting "Bubbles!" to perk yourself back up and regain emotional control, two things will happen: (1) You will regain emotional control because no one can stay in a bad mood attempting to shout "Bubbles!" Go ahead. Try it. I'll wait. (2) Your co-workers or family are going to be far less likely to fuck with you because you are rage-screaming "Bubbles!" at the side of the building or dwelling you're in.

Final reminder, no one is expecting you to walk away from a tense situation or awkward confrontation for twenty minutes and come back as chipper as if it never happened. Being emotionally mature does not mean you are suppressing your emotions. Nope, you're probably going to come back to that encounter annoyed or frustrated. But annoyed or frustrated and in control of that. You can be regulated and still feel a feeling. You're just not on the edge of losing it again. And if you have to reenter that confrontational space, you may have to repeat the process. That's okay. We are humans and brains can be very unfair with the emotional deployment.

FIELD GUIDE ENTRY: *Gentle Partnering*

The jokes are eternal.

"How many kids do you have?" "Three, plus a husband. So, basically four."

"You've got two kids, right?" "Three. My wife gave birth to two and acts like a third."

I'm gonna be up-front; partner infantilization and poop jokes carry the same energy for me. I don't like either.

There is an entire chapter dedicated to splitting the difference in responsively raising children with slightly different approaches. ("Peanut Butter & Jelly," just in case you're cherry-picking the chapters here. No judgment. Read how you want. I'm just glad you're reading it.) But what about when your partner needs all that same education and mental training? What happens when you have been really working on understanding your feelings and where your breaking points are but your partner is still floating off in a primordial ooze of reactive outbursts and emotional immaturity?

The answer is not responsively parenting them too. You can't responsively parent folks who aren't your children. This is especially true of your partner, spouse, husband, wife, life mate, helpmeet, whatever you want to call that person you share life and/or offspring with.

Your partner might need practice with emotional regulation, and your relationship may greatly benefit from viewing their emotional development the same as you view that of the children you share. But you're not parenting them. You are partnering them. That's a weird verb to choose here but I'm not gonna find a different one. The work you put into an adult who is just sort of mastering this whole emotionally responsive and available and communicative gig is still not a child. They are a grown adult with, hopefully, all their brain bits fully online. They aren't having to define *and* learn how to regulate all the different flavors of feelings.

That's going to be the bigger divider between gentle parenting and gentle partnering. Children aren't just learning what to do with their feelings. They are learning what those feelings feel like and how to differentiate between them. An adult can most likely process the difference between annoyed and frustrated and exhausted. A child still needs that hand-holding to know if they are struggling with the internal rage monster because they are just tired, or if they are really annoyed at the situation. So as your partner learns how to identify their emotions, it's more about identifying their triggers than the actual mechanics and definition of the feeling.

And remember, it starts with you. The process of being able to identify triggers, name your feelings, and decide what you need to do to feel them safely and without making it everyone else's problem starts with work you do on yourself. The same is going to have to be true for your partner. You can help. You can be patient. You can even call them on their bullshit when they are beyond dysregulated and beginning to melt down. But you can't parent them. Why? Because they are not your kid.

FIELD GUIDE ENTRY:
Responsive Aunties and Funcles

I love gentle aunts and uncles. Any sort of attention paid to a child's emotional development is a net positive. Hopefully the siblings that are raising your niblings are also doing responsive parenting or some version of it. But if they are not, there are still roles you can play in this.

As a reminder, you cannot responsively parent a child that is not yours. You can be supportive. You can help them define, identify, regulate, and work with feelings when they are with you. But ultimately that child's development lands on the shoulders of your sibling. And that can be so damn hard to swallow, especially if you are seeing mistakes your parents made be repeated with your nieces and nephews.

If those littles you love so much are not being raised in any sort of authoritative or intentional manner, you'll have a lot longer time frame on those regulations. That's okay. Children thrive on consistency. You're going to be the odd one out for a bit. But they also absolutely flourish in environments wherein they are allowed to experience emotion without repercussion. If you are that space for them, even better.

TL;DR

You can use responsive parenting techniques on your asshole boss or annoying co-worker. You cannot parent humans that aren't your children. Gwenna is okay at verbs.

· 23 ·

CO-REGULATION APPENDIX

Regulation is not the same as suppression. You aren't trying to stop the tantrum. You're giving them ways to calm down. Dr. Kristyn Sommer describes the anatomy of a tantrum as an arc. There's a windup, cresting up to a full-blown meltdown, and then a cooldown. You can talk feelings during the windup and cooldown. But at peak fit, communication isn't gonna happen. They can't hear you. And they definitely won't remember what you were trying to say, 'cuz brain chemical things.

So as a responsive parent, we are hoping to lessen the number of tantrums by helping them identify their feelings before the break. As they feel themselves climbing up Tantrum Mountain with time, practice, and repetition, they come to a point where they can identify they are about to lose it and reign it back in. This isn't to say they don't still feel frustrated or angry or sad, but they don't melt down as a result of being overwhelmed by those emotions. But that, like all other things in childhood and humanhood for that matter, takes time and practice to get good at. Even so, the best, most emotionally aware and regulated humans still lose their shit.

So what are you supposed to do in the times that the emotional awareness schtick doesn't work and a tantrum erupts? The answer that really kinda sucks is . . . you have to ride it out. You can regulate with them. If you haven't lost your shit yet, you can demonstrate ways to talk yourself off the ledge, metaphorically speaking.

More bad news incoming, I'm afraid. There is no one way to regulate. What works for child A will send child B into complete hysterics. What worked for child C last time seems to be making it worse this time. There are a ton of different ways to regulate, and for the third time in this book, we're talking artisanal spaghetti. Grab some co-regulation noodles that look kinda okay and find a wall.

However, and this is the really important part, you need to get it out of your head that it's your job as a responsive parent to stop the tantrum. Nope. You aren't trying to end it, you're trying to help them calm themselves back down.

But Gwenna, that sounds like the same thing. You're just splitting hairs at this point.

Okay, fair point. Let's do a thought experiment here. Think about the last time you were really riled up: angry tears, visions of illegal actions dancing through your head, hands quivering with the need to throw something, barely keeping your voice below a roar, "Mother, I crave violence" kind of mad. Now imagine, in the midst of your trying to keep yourself out of prison, someone looks at you and says, "Now just calm down." Even in this hypothetical space, you kinda want to donkey-kick someone's throat, right?

When a parent, at their rope's emotionally frayed end, tries to stop a tantrum, no matter what words they choose, the effect is the same. "Just calm down" ain't gonna do shit. Chances are pretty great it's gonna make it worse. It would for you, a grown adult in possession of a fully developed brain. Same goes for the kiddo in meltdown mode.

Back to pissed-off imaginary you. You've got all the big, seeing-red feels swimming around your cortisol-soaked gray matter. Now imagine someone gives you a smile, hands you a bowl of your cherished comfort food or a nice warm mug of your favorite hot beverage, and sits quietly with you, occasionally whispering, "It's okay. I'm here when you're ready. You're safe. You can be mad. Let it out." Whole different effect in this scenario.

Your feelings weren't invalidated. You weren't told to cut it out and suck it up. No one pressured you into wrapping this whole fit throwing up so we can all move on with our day. You were given space, time, and support to process. And even in that completely made-up situation, I'd wager you felt calmer much quicker.

That's a co-regulation. Again, it works the same way with the kiddos. It just takes a little longer 'cuz their little brains are good at feeling big things, not excellent at coming back down off those emotional highs. (Remember that emotional self-regulation is controlled by the prefrontal cortex that doesn't come online fully until your early to mid-twenties.) By practicing co-regulation with our kids, we are essentially loaning them the little voice in our heads that keeps us from murdering people who bring forty-three items to the ten-items-or-less checkout aisle.

Here's what keeps me from losing my shit when my kids

lose theirs. It's not our job to prevent our kids from the big, bad, ugly feelings. If anything our job is to give them permission to feel those things and pave ways to walk themselves back to level ground. You aren't failing this whole parenting gig if your kid is pissed off. I'd venture to say you're doing it right.

In Disney's *Finding Nemo,* Marlon is a suppressive parent with the best of intentions. One poignant scene includes this exchange.

> **Marlon:** I promised I would never let anything happen to him.
>
> **Dory:** Well, that's silly 'cuz then nothing would ever happen to him.

Teaching our kids how to deal with adversity does not mean we are preventing adversity. It means acknowledging it, embracing that it will happen however unpleasant and poorly timed, and demonstrating ways to cope successfully. It starts when they are little and the worst thing that has ever happened in their two whole years of life is that the bowl is red, not blue.

By allowing them to feel mad about the wrong color bowl, giving them space to freak out, and helping them come back down to a space where they can accept that the red bowl holds Goldfish just as well as the blue bowl, we are giving them the earliest forms of skills they'll use later when the problems get bigger, more complex, and harder to grapple with.

Now, in the case of the red versus the blue bowl, I'm not advocating hard-lining the battle of the bowl. Sometimes a parent has to choose the battle. If you're willing and able to wash the blue bowl and can do so for the sake of not having a meltdown, do it. Not every moment has to be a teachable moment. But if you've got the mental energy and emotional space to address the bowl thing, do it.

What follows is a wildly incomplete list of co-regulation techniques you can try. Some of these will work sometimes. Some of these might become go-tos. Some of these will piss your child off even more and should never be attempted more than once. But if you've got an arsenal of ways to help your child come out of the rage stratosphere, you'll feel a little more in control of both yourself and the situation.

As you're reading through, remember the tantrum arc.

These tools are deployed at breakdown and at peak tantrum point. Any sort of communication about the problem or the tantrum itself won't and, biochemically speaking, can't be heard past the point of buildup and before the cooldown period. If you get to the point of your child having a breakdown, you are in co-regulation territory.

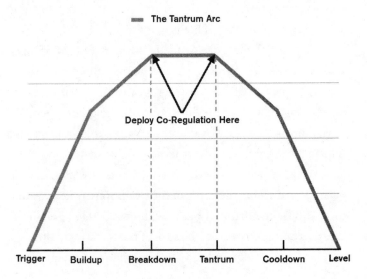

The Tantrum Arc

Deploy Co-Regulation Here

Trigger   Buildup   Breakdown   Tantrum   Cooldown   Level

Final disclaimer: It's never too early to begin teaching consent. Some of these require physical contact and some kids really don't want to be touched, especially when already pissed off. Unless I need to physically move my child out of danger or into a space where they can continue their meltdown without ruining the dining experience of others in the packed Chili's, I ask if they want to do any of these things and respect their "no." That looks like this script:

"Wow, you are all the mad? Do you want a hug? A cuddle? Do you want to hold my hand? Okay, well, I'm going to go get a drink. I'll get you some water."

Some days my kids are down for regulatory touches. Sometimes I ask and they respond as if I'd asked if I could light the dog on fire. All the same, I'm not gonna violate that touch boundary they are allowed to set unless their physical safety or the well-being of others is at risk.

Space Cadet: Stay within eye and earshot of the tantrum. Keep your body language and expression as neutral as possible. Get to their level, wherever that is. Sit on the floor or couch and just wait it out. You don't have to stare them down or say anything at all. Just zone out. Show that you can be calm in the midst of chaos. But by keeping your energy level, kids often match that and begin to calm themselves down.

Gentle Touch: This can look like a lot of things: back pats, belly rubs, playing with their hair, stroking their arm, rubbing their hands, finger taps, hand-holding, just letting them sit in your lap while they cry. Provide some point of physical contact while they let out the worst of it.

Scream It Out: This is the opposite of Space Cadet but does require just a bit of notice. As tempting as it is, I don't recommend just screaming back in their face. Will that make you feel better? Probably. Might not do much for the tantrum though. Tell them you think screaming is a good idea and that you might just join them. Alternatively, ask if you can scream too. And then, do it. Scream it out. Maybe let a few of your big feels out while you do.

Playful Touches: This is similar to gentle touches but adding tickles, wiggles, funny kisses, thumb wars, hand keep-away. A physical point of contact that can also be perceived as a game.

Deep Contact: Scoop your kids up in a big bear hug and squeeze tight gently. Face them away from you so their spine is toward your front. Wrap them up so that your legs are over theirs and your arms cross over their chest. Put your face down next to theirs if you're that type of bendy. You are now their deep-pressure weighted blanket. Do this move with caution and only when you are in control of your own emotional state. You're not aiming for any level of pain or discomfort, you are aiming to apply deep and enveloping pressure and get all those fiery nerve-endings of your tantrumming offspring to feel less like they are on fire.

The Spot™: When not in the middle of a tantrum, work with your kid to establish a spot in the house. It might be their bed, a corner of floor in the closet, the bathtub, whatever works for you and your family. This spot is where they can go and feel all their big feels securely. You might add a pillow, a weighted blanket, a lavender-scented thing, a book or two. Stay within earshot of The Spot.

Make 'Em Laugh: This is a go-to in the Laithland house. The minute I can get someone to laugh, I know the tantrum is wrapping up. Whatever makes your kid laugh is the thing to try. My littles are sadistic so any inkling of someone falling over, stumbling, tripping, dropping something, or taking a hit is comedy gold to them. I have dropped many an empty plastic tumbler for the sake of a tantrum-ending gag.

Emotional Support Redirect: If your child has a lovey or a comfort item like a blankie, when the fit is starting to really take root and settle, ask them to go get their lovey for emotional support. If they don't come with a pre-assigned lovey from the factory, you may be able to suggest a favorite stuffy, doll, action figure, or toy in its place.

Helpful Henry: This blends Space Cadet with a redirect and poking their funny bone. Grab an item (preferably one that, if thrown, won't hurt or be hurt) and ask them just to hold it. Then go grab another. And another. Increase your speed and urgency as you go. Eventually you'll end up with a heap of stuff balanced on your child and they are likely to have disengaged that part of their brain that makes rational thought hard. Now they are invested in what the hell are you doing and why am I holding all this stuff?

Shared Emotion: While not my personal favorite, some kids respond really well to knowing they are not the only one feeling a feel. On the edge of crying yourself? Let the tears flow. Are you mad too? Let them see how to be mad without making it everyone else's problem.

Breathing Techniques: This one encompasses a lot of different techniques. Everything from simply taking big, deep breaths to more controlled breathing exercises count.

Circular Breathing: In through the nose, out through the mouth.

Measured Breathing: Plug one nostril, breathe in. Release nostril, plug other nostril, breathe out.

Square Breaths: Breathe in for a count of four, hold for a count of four, breathe out for a count of four, hold for a count of four.

Audible Breathing: Big, deep breath in, release as you let your voice do whatever. Ahh, hmm, pterodactyl screech. Whatever feels right in the moment.

Ha Ha Ha: Big deep breath in, release with short, loud *ha ha ha*s until you're out of air.

Shaky Ribs: Take the biggest breath you possibly can and then take in more air. Try to open your ribs and press your diaphragm so far down your tummy starts to shake or quiver. Release it all in a big whoosh. Repeat.

Rainbow Breathing: Start with your arms at your side. As you inhale through your mouth, keep your arms straight and lift your hands over your head. As you exhale, let your arms fall back to your sides. It should look like you made a big rainbow with your arms.

Head, Shoulders, Knees, and Toes: Remember that song from childhood? "Head, shoulders, knees and toes, knees and toes"? That one. Yep. Turns out this is an excellent regulation technique. Just start singing the song and doing the little dancey dance. If that doesn't do it for you, pick another song that has motions and repetition. Anything that will encourage physical motion in your emotionally tapped small human. Will this look like standing in front of your screaming child dancing like a circus clown? Yes. If it feels like nonsense but it works, is it still nonsense?

Run a Lap: Pent-up energy has to come out. If it's pouring out emotionally, sometimes you can switch the tap by going for a jog. Or a skip. Or a walk. Or do jumping jacks. Get physical, get moving, and get moving on from the breakdown.

Stimming: Stims got a bad rap while Gen X and millennials were growing up. Even as our society shifted to a more accepting and aware state where mental health was concerned, stimming still felt like only a thing for autistic people. Not true. Most humans stim in some way. Some are more subtle and others require the self-regulation of a stim way more often, but most humans stim. When your kid is in the middle of a tantrum, demonstrate your favorite stims: rocking, hand claps, finger taps, hand wiggles, toe lifts, calf raises, face or head rubbing, arm flapping, turning in circles, buzz lips, wringing of hands, humming or cooing sounds. Any sort of action or motion that scratches that itchy spot in your brain, do that, and encourage them to try it. If you already know what your child's preferred stims are, demonstrate those or verbally remind them they can use those stims.

Sensory Counting: A grounding technique used by actual professionals in therapy settings, this one works as a regulation technique as well. Activate your child's senses by asking them to help you find five things you can see, four things you can touch, three things you can hear, two things you can smell, one thing you can taste. If this is one of the first times you are trying this, you can simply walk through the exercise yourself where they can see and hear you. Then you can invite them to help you locate those things. Finally, it will evolve to simply asking them to find the five, four, three, two, one, and they are regulating.

Alphabet Soup: Related to sensory counting, this one works really well if you're trapped in the tantrum space like the car or a public bathroom you hid in when your child started melting down in public (no judgment, we've all done it). Start naming things you see that start with letters of the alphabet. Can't find a thing that starts with *A*, pick a random letter and go from there. *A* is for air freshener. *B* is for baby wipes. *C* is for cold water. It's not an exact science. A few letters in you can invite the kid to join the game. Don't stress if they don't get it right. You and I both know that "toilet" doesn't start with *P* but now's not the time for an alphabet lesson. Let it ride.

Bubbles: A long time ago on an internet of ages past there was a meme that factually stated there is no way to say the word "bubbles" angrily. Try it. Try to say "bubbles" in a mad voice. Doesn't work. Don't know why. I imagine it's quite a sight when my kid is entering a tantrum in public and I just start shouting, "Bubbles! Bubbles! BUBBLES!" at her. She typically tries shouting "Bubbles!" back and when she can't sound mad anymore, it helps her not feel quite so overwhelmed by said mad.

Lip Farts: Purse your lips, force air through them to make the fart sound. You can also stick your tongue out and blow raspberries. Children seem to be universally amused by fart noises. Lean into that. Give them something else to focus on while the tantrum works its way out of their system.

Write It Down: If your small human has already mastered the written language, you can encourage them to write down what they are feeling and why. Writing engages a different part of our brain and helps us disengage from the part that is overwhelmed with the big feel.

Once again, this is not a complete list. And it won't all work for your kid at any given point. That just means you have to find more spaghetti to throw at that wall. If you're having to start from scratch, start with you. If you're in an okay mood, what will instantly swing you into a good mood? Chances are pretty great that that same thing will help move you from a bad mood to at least an okay mood.

The more you practice these co-regulations with your kid, the more they'll begin to internalize these methods and apply them to their own regulation process. While my anecdotal evidence does not represent all of humanity, my eldest, a teenager at the time of this writing, no longer requires co-regulation. Occasionally I'll need to cue her that she's getting amped and might need a second, but she can recognize her own emotional state getting elevated and takes the steps her body and mind require to cool off.

She is capable of regulating herself probably five of ten times. I don't have to get involved beyond asking her if she needs to take a moment. And I know, a 50 percent failure rate is atrocious. But she's fourteen and I've only been focused on her emotional health and wellness for six to seven years. Remember, I wasn't always a responsive parent. But we got there. You'll get there, too.

AFTERWORD

You've got this.

No, don't argue with a book.

You've got this. I know you do.

How do I know you've got this?

For starters, you've reached the end of this book.

You've read or listened to an entire book with hopes to learn something, feel better about your parenting choices, find some peace, or make some sense of how not to fuck your kids up.

Parents who don't care, who aren't trying, don't do shit like that.

I'll give you this. This book was kind of a lot, huh? I'm betting there were times you cheered (silently, in your head), or more likely nodded emphatically. You probably deeply related to some of the stories and anecdotes because something nearly identical happened to you while parenting in the wild. You felt my pain because you've felt the same.

There may have been times you felt a little attacked. Or maybe overwhelmed. I've never, ever read a parenting book that didn't make me feel at least a little guilty in some way or another. I'm guessing it was the same for you. Phrases you muttered, grumbled, or thought may have included:

"I should have known that."

"Oh shit, I've done that."

"Lower your voice when you call me out like that, Gwenna."

For those moments, I am sorry. That sucks. You picked up a book thinking you'd get some nice little tidbits of info that might make raising your crop of womb fruit a little easier, and instead feel bullied by words on paper. Remember, there's Mom Guilt and there's Mom Shame. Which was tugging at you in those moments? Because that makes a difference.

I hope you related. I hope you laughed. I hope you had a light bulb click on at least once or twice. Ultimately I hope you walk away from this book feeling just a little more in control of your feelings, a little more capable of being a great parent, and a little more confident that you've got this.

Because you do. You really, really do. You're doing okay. And okay is the best most of us can hope for on any given day. The great days, the banner days—those are rare. Most of our days, whether we are parents or child-free, are just okay. We can celebrate the okay days. They are better and more prefera-ble than the bad ones, at least.

I've said it a billion times on the internet and I'll joyfully say it a billion more times. You're a good parent. You are. First, you read a parenting book. Willingly. Because I'm doubting this thing will ever be used in a college course on parenting ideol-ogy. If it ends up in a college course it will be as a sociological exploration of bad millennial jokes. But not for parenting.

So I can say, without a doubt, you chose to read this book. You kept with it. Bad parents don't do shit like that. Bad parents never wonder if they are doing a good job. Good parents never stop worrying that they're doing a bad one.

You're doing your best. And that's enough.

I opened this book stating there's no such thing as a parenting expert. That's as true now as it was then. Who's the only expert available on raising your child?

Yep. You got it.

You. You're the parent your child needs. And you're doing great. I promise.

—Gwenna

AUTHOR'S NOTE

I f you've read all the way through this book you may have noticed a distinct lack of reference to or resources described specifically for special-needs parents. I rarely if ever acknowledged kids with special needs, littles on any of the neurodivergent spectrums, children with developmental delays or neurological diseases, kids with communication differences or high support needs, or a host of other instances where the standard parenting rhetoric may not apply.

No, I don't reference you or your kids in this book because, simply put, I can't. Not with any authority or confidence, at least. Some of the content absolutely may apply to your parenting situation, with or without modification. But some of it may not because of the unique circumstances in which you and your children exist. This was done intentionally and not maliciously. I wrote this book based on my personal experiences and a whole lot of overthinking stuff. This means that my experience raising kids as described above is not just limited, it is absent. Essentially this is the recognition of my lane and my best attempt to stay in it. I don't want you to feel left out of this examination of one possible way to raise good humans. I do want to clarify that I'm not in the business of misinformation. If I don't know (and there's a lot I don't know), I'm going to say I don't know. And when it comes to parenting kids with developmental delays or differences, I don't know.

If something you read in this book seems applicable but you might need to alter a few bits, do it. Bring it up with your care team, your physicians, your specialists, and your therapists. Discuss. Find the ways that work for you and your family if you've found an idea you'd like to apply but it won't work as I've described it here. For the final time, you are the best expert on your kid. You're the parenting expert here. Not me.

ACKNOWLEDGMENTS

*Never would I have ever believed that I was
gonna actually write a book. I decided to
give a lot of consideration to those of
you who spent countless hours helping me
up and out of the doldrums of writing.
Never could I forget to thank my mom who is
gonna read every word of this book when I
let her read the whole thing already.
You never let me forget who I was or let me get
down on myself. To my husband who was
never hesitant to hear a new passage, I'm never
gonna be sorry for asking you for validation or to
run out my biggest hang-ups with a hug. You're
around my best and worst and love them both.
And you helped me learn to fly and will never
desert me. I have faith and confidence that
you are one of the best gifts in my life. I'm*

never going to take that for granted. You are
gonna be my biggest cheerleader, and you always
make it easier to pursue my dreams. I love
you. To my friends who routinely make me
cry with their unending love and support . . .
never stop being you. Never stop being true.
Gonna have to wrap this up, but let me just
say a support network makes all the difference.
Goodbye to the doubts. Farewell loneliness. I'm
never gonna tell a lie and hurt you.

And because I believe no one actually reads these:

For those of you who did, you've been Rickrolled. Reread the first word of each line. I'm not sorry. Because I am, at my core, a millennial. Actual acknowledgments are: Big props to my agents, Wendy & Callie. Thanks for all the handholding. And to Eileen, who saw through my imposter syndrome immediately. Thanks, Mom, B, A, S, E, T, E, L, & R.

Oh, and you lost the game.

INDEX

ABOUT THE AUTHOR

GWENNA LAITHLAND was born and raised in Oklahoma. Gwenna got her start as a writer at the age of eighteen. She branched out into content marketing soon after and has worked with museums, professional sports teams, accounting firms, and universities to help refine their content. She started *Momma Cusses* in 2019, first as an e-zine, then shifted toward a social media focus in 2020. She still lives in Oklahoma with her husband and three kids.